COMPLETE GUIDE TO BASIC PROGRAMMING

QB64

Olanrewaju Sanni

This book is dedicated to the Almighty.

INTRODUCTION

Complete Guide to BASIC Programming: QB64

How BASIC Made Its Way into the 21st Century

The **BASIC** language has been a gateway into programming for countless individuals. Popular as a beginner's programming language in the '80s, it evolved into a powerful professional tool in the '90s. BASIC, along with its successor **QBasic**, ignited a love for programming in many, providing the foundational learning platform for today's professional developers.

But what if we could bring the magic of BASIC from its 20th-century roots into the modern era? Enter the **QB64** project —a remarkable evolution over the last decade. **QB64** retains compatibility with **QBasic/QuickBASIC 4.5** while adding a host of extensions. Here's why it's a game-changer:

1. **Automatic Compilation**: Unlike traditional BASIC and QBasic code, QB64 compiles automatically into machine code. This means exceptional performance, easy distribution, and the ability to link with external C and C++ libraries.

2. **Classic Meets Modern**: QB64 seamlessly blends classic and modern program development. It's compatible with most QBasic 4.5 code and adds features like **OpenGL** and other contemporary enhancements.

3. **Educational and Professional**: QB64 is already in use across educational and professional contexts. Its active and helpful user community ensures continuous growth and support.

4. **Cross-Platform**: Available for recent versions of

Windows, **Linux**, and **macOS**, QB64 empowers programmers regardless of their operating system.

Who Created QB64?

For a glimpse into QB64's early history, check out the interviews with its creators. Their vision has transformed BASIC from a nostalgic relic into a dynamic language for the 21st century.

Whether you're a seasoned developer or a curious beginner, QB64 invites you to explore the intersection of tradition and innovation. Dive into the world of QB64 codes and unlock your programming potential!

Getting Started - QB64

QBasic and **QB64** are user-friendly computer languages that are easy to learn. They are both freely available and compatible with most computers. This book will help you begin your programming journey in QBasic and QB64.

QB64 Download

www.qb64.org

Navigating QB64 Environment

Navigating the QB64 software is essential for efficient programming. Let's explore how to get around:

Installation and Setup:

1. First, ensure you have installed QB64 on your system.

If not, follow the instructions provided on the official QB64 website1.

2. Next, download the tutorial asset file (if you haven't already) and place the "tutorial" folder in your QB64 installation directory.

Launching QB64:

1. Run the QB64 executable to open the Integrated Development Environment (IDE).

2. You can use the IDE to edit your .BAS files.

Compiling and Running Code:

1. To compile and run your code, press F5.

2. If you want to generate a binary without running it, press F11.

Explore and Experiment:

Dive into the lessons, experiment with code, and discover the power of QB64.

Remember, every line of code tells a story. Let QB64 be your canvas, and let the adventure begin!

CHAPTER 1 - FIRST PROGRAM

Sample 1

CLS

PRINT "Hello From QB64"

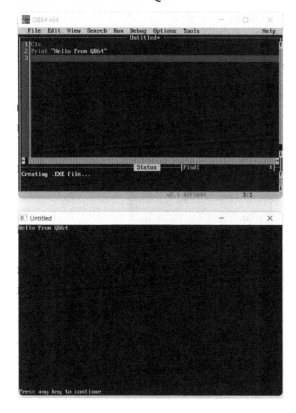

Sample 2

CLS

PRINT "Hello QB64"

PRINT "Hello World"

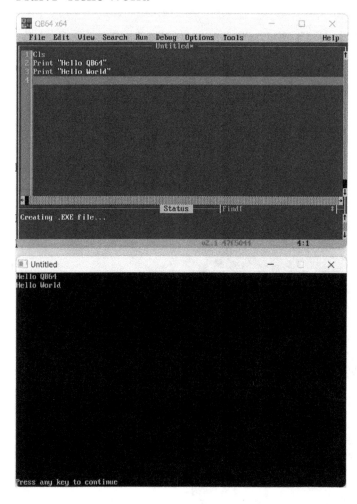

CHAPTER 2 - PRINTING MATH - QB64

In Chapter 1, we explored how the PRINT statement could display text enclosed in quotes. But did you know that PRINT can do more than just handle plain text? It's also capable of printing calculations!

In the world of **QBasic/QB64**, we adhere to the math rule of **PEMDAS** (Parentheses, Exponents, Multiplication and Division, Addition and Subtraction).

> **P**arentheses

> **E**xponents

> **M**ultiplication

> **D**ivision

> **A**ddition

> **S**ubtraction

This order of operations ensures that expressions are evaluated correctly.

So, whether you're printing a simple message or performing complex calculations, remember that **PRINT** is your versatile companion in the world of **BASIC programming**!

Functions Used in This Chapter:

1. **SQR:** This function calculates the square root of a given value.

2. ABS: The ABS function returns the absolute value (magnitude) of a number.

Sample Code

```
CLS

PRINT 15 + 3

PRINT 42 - 5

PRINT 4 * 36

PRINT 15 / 5

PRINT 4 ^ 3

PRINT SQR(64)

PRINT ABS(-3)

PRINT 15 * 3 + 42

PRINT (15 * 3) + 42

PRINT 15 * (3 + 42)
```

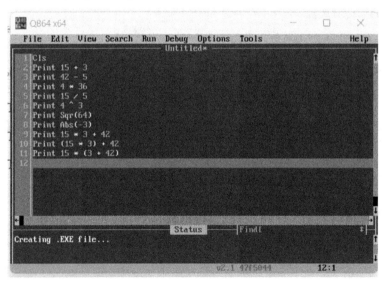

CHAPTER 3 - PRINT FORMATTING - QB64

In this chapter, print formatting will be used to show the user what calculations are being used to get the results.

When working with QBasic/QB64, it's essential to use separators between strings and calculations. These separators serve different purposes:

1. **Comma (,):** The comma aligns output in columns. It's useful for creating neatly formatted tables or lists. For example:

PRINT "Name", "Age", "Score"

PRINT "Alice", 25, 90

PRINT "Bob", 30, 85

2. **Semicolon (;):** The semicolon keeps output adjacent to each other without adding extra spaces. It's suitable for displaying information side by side. For example:

PRINT "Hello"; "World"; "!"

Sample Code 1

Here's an example of how you can use separators in QBasic/QB64 to display output with calculations:

CLS

PRINT "QB", "Tutorial", "5"

```
PRINT "QB "; "Tutorial "; "5"
PRINT "Calculation:"; 6 + 5
```

When you run this code, it will produce the following output:

```
QB     Tutorial      5
QB Tutorial 5
Calculation: 11
```

Sample Code 2

```
CLS
PRINT "10 + 10 ="; 10 + 10
PRINT "11 - 5 ="; 11 - 5
PRINT "7 * 8 ="; 7 * 8
PRINT "10 / 5 ="; 10 / 5
PRINT "3 Power 3 ="; 3^3
PRINT "Square Root Of 81 ="; SQR(81)
PRINT "The Absolute Value -8 ="; ABS(-8)
PRINT "5 * 2 + 12 ="; 5 * 2 + 12
PRINT "(5 * 5) + 15 ="; (5 * 5) + 15
PRINT "5 * (6 + 12) ="; 5 * (6 + 12)
```

When you run this code, it will produce the following output:

```
10 + 10 = 20
11 - 5 = 6
7 * 8 = 56
10 / 5 = 2.0
```

3 Power 3 = 27

Square Root Of 81 = 9.0

The Absolute Value -8 = 8

5 * 2 + 12 = 22

(5 * 5) + 15 = 40

5 * (6 + 12) = 90

Feel free to adjust the strings and calculations as needed for your specific program.

CHAPTER 4 - VARIABLES AND DATA TYPES - QB64

Data Types in QBasic / QB64

When programming, the computer needs to store and manage data in memory. To do this effectively, the programmer specifies the **data type**, which defines the kind of data the computer will handle. Here are the common data types in QBasic/QB64:

1. **String**: Represents text and characters. For example:

This line is an example of a string.

2. **Integer**: Stores non-floating-point numbers within the range of -32,768 to 32,767. Examples:

67, -34, -100, 203, 1022, -1, 0

3. **Long**: Holds non-floating-point numbers within the range of -2,147,483,648 to 2,147,483,647. Examples:

560005, 3, -2, 0, -867000, 14, 8, -10

4. **Single**: Represents floating-point numbers with a wide range from approximately -3.37x10^38 to 3.37x10^38. Examples:

4.3, 25.4567, -35.87, 0.35, -3.14

5. **Double**: Stores floating-point numbers with an even larger range from approximately -1.67x10^308 to

1.67x10^308. Examples:

745663.90596, -98.12, 4859903.094491

For a comprehensive list of QB64 data types, you can refer to the QB64 Wiki.

Variables

Variables are essential for holding data in memory during program execution. Here are some key points about variables:

- Variables are assigned a data type.
- The data stored in variables can change throughout the program.
- The entered data must match the assigned data type.

Two ways to declare variables in QBasic/QB64:

1. **Using Data Type Symbols After the Name**:

MyName$ ' String

Num1%   ' Integer

Num2!   ' Single

Answer# ' Double

2. **Using DIM (Preferred Method)**:

DIM MyName AS STRING

DIM Num1 AS INTEGER

DIM Num2 AS SINGLE

DIM Answer AS DOUBLE

Remember that variable names should not start with a number or a character that is not a letter. Additionally, avoid using reserved names like PRINT, INPUT, LET, ABS, BEEP, etc. as variable name.

Sample Code 1

```
CLS

Header$ = "This is an example program"
Num1% = 10
Num2% = 15
Num3& = 60000
Num4& = 72000
Num5! = 5.5
Num6! = 8.25
Num7# = 70000.5
Num8# = 95000.67

PRINT Header$
PRINT Num1% + Num2% + Num3&
PRINT Num6! / Num5!
PRINT Num8# + Num2%
PRINT Num4& / Num1%
```

When you run this code, it will produce the following output:

This is an example program

60025

1.5

95015.67

7200

Feel free to adjust the strings and calculations as needed for your specific program.

Sample Code 2

```
DIM Num1 AS INTEGER
DIM Num2 AS LONG
DIM Num3 AS SINGLE
DIM Num4 AS DOUBLE
DIM Header AS STRING

CLS

Header = "This is another example"
Num1 = 10
Num2 = 72000
Num3 = 55.235
Num4 = 85000.1234

PRINT Header
PRINT Num1 + Num2 + Num3 + Num4
```

When you run this code, it will produce the following output:

This is another example

157065.3584

Feel free to adjust the strings and calculations as needed for your specific program.

CHAPTER 5 - TYPE MISMATCH AND OTHER DATA TYPE ERRORS - QB64

In programming, it is crucial to ensure that the **data type** of a variable matches the expected type. If there is a mismatch, it can lead to unexpected behavior. Here are a couple of scenarios to illustrate this:

1. **Type Mismatch with Numeric Data:**
   - Suppose the computer expects an **integer** (whole number) but receives a **floating-point number** (decimal). In such cases, the computer may automatically round the floating-point value to the nearest integer.
   - For example, if the expected variable type is an integer, and we assign the value 3.14 (a floating-point number), the computer might round it to 3.

2. **Variable Name Typos:**
   - If a variable's name is misspelled or does not match the original variable name, the computer will create a **new variable** with the incorrect name.
   - This new variable will be **initialized** with a

default value (often zero) based on its data type.

Remember, paying attention to data types and variable names helps prevent subtle bugs and ensures smooth execution of your code!

Sample Code 1

```
DIM Title AS STRING
CLS
Title = "New Title"
PRINT Title
```

When you run this code, it will produce the following output:

Title

Sample Code 2

```
DIM Title AS STRING
CLS
Title = 30
PRINT Title
```

This program will produce the following output:

Type mismatch or illegal string-number conversion

Sample Code 3

```
DIM Title AS STRING
DIM x AS INTEGER
CLS
```

```
Title = "Tutorial 5"
x = 50
PRINT Title
PRINT x
```

Let's break it down:

1. DIM Title AS STRING: This line declares a variable named Title with the data type STRING. It allocates memory for storing a string value.

2. DIM x AS INTEGER: Here, a variable named x is declared with the data type INTEGER. It reserves memory for an integer value.

3. CLS: The CLS command clears the screen or console, removing any previous output.

4. Title = "Tutorial 5": The value "Tutorial 5" is assigned to the Title variable.

5. x = 50: The integer value 50 is assigned to the x variable.

6. PRINT Title: This line prints the value of the Title variable (which is "Tutorial 5") to the console.

7. PRINT x: Similarly, it prints the value of the x variable (which is 50).

The output of the provided BASIC code snippet would be:

```
Tutorial 5
50
```

Explanation:

The PRINT Title statement displays the value of the Title variable, which is "Tutorial 5".

The PRINT x statement shows the value of the x variable, which is 50.

Sample Code 4

DIM Title AS STRING

DIM x AS INTEGER

CLS

Title = "Best Title"

x = "Gist"

PRINT Title

PRINT x

Let's analyze the provided QB64 code step by step:

1. **DIM Title AS STRING:**
   - This line declares a variable named Title with the data type STRING.
   - **No error here.**

2. **DIM x AS INTEGER:**
   - This line declares a variable named x with the data type INTEGER.
   - **No error here.**

3. **CLS:**
   - The CLS command clears the screen or console, removing any previous output.
   - **No error here.**

4. **Title = "Best Title":**
   - The value "Best Title" is assigned to the Title variable.

◦ **No error here.**

5. **x = "Gist":**

    ◦ **ERROR: Type mismatch!**

    ◦ **The variable x is declared as an INTEGER, but we are assigning a STRING value ("Gist").**

    ◦ **QB64 does not allow assigning a string value to an integer variable.**

6. **PRINT Title:**

    ◦ This line prints the value of the Title variable (which is "Best Title").

    ◦ **No error here.**

7. **PRINT x:**

    ◦ **ERROR: Type mismatch!**

    ◦ **The variable x contains a string value ("Gist"), but it is declared as an INTEGER.**

    ◦ **QB64 does not allow printing a string value stored in an integer variable.**

To fix this, either change the data type of x to STRING or assign an integer value to it. For example:

```
DIM Title AS STRING

DIM x AS STRING ' Change to STRING data type

CLS

Title = "Best Title"

x = "Gist"

PRINT Title

PRINT x
```

This modified code will correctly handle the string assignment and printing.

Sample Code 5

```
DIM Title AS STRING
DIM x AS INTEGER
CLS
Title = "Tutorial 5"
x = 50.25
PRINT Title
PRINT x
```

Let's analyze the provided QB64 code step by step:

1. **DIM Title AS STRING:**
    - This line declares a variable named Title with the data type STRING.
    - **No error here.**

2. **DIM x AS INTEGER:**
    - This line declares a variable named x with the data type INTEGER.
    - **No error here.**

3. **CLS:**
    - The CLS command clears the screen or console, removing any previous output.
    - **No error here.**

4. **Title = "Tutorial 5":**
    - The value "Tutorial 5" is assigned to the Title variable.
    - **No error here.**

5. **x = 50.25:**
   - ERROR: Type mismatch!
   - **The variable x is declared as an INTEGER, but we are assigning a FLOATING-POINT value (50.25).**
   - **QB64 does not allow assigning a floating-point value to an integer variable.**

6. **PRINT Title:**
   - This line prints the value of the Title variable (which is "Tutorial 5").
   - **No error here.**

7. **PRINT x:**
   - ERROR: Type mismatch!
   - **The variable x contains a floating-point value (50.25), but it is declared as an INTEGER.**
   - **QB64 does not allow printing a floating-point value stored in an integer variable.**

To fix this, either change the data type of x to FLOAT or assign an integer value to it. For example:

```
DIM Title AS STRING
DIM x AS FLOAT  ' Change to FLOAT data type
CLS
Title = "Tutorial 5"
x = 50
PRINT Title
PRINT x
```

This modified code will correctly handle the string assignment and printing.

Sample Code 6

```
DIM x AS STRING
DIM y AS INTEGER
CLS
x = "First Title"
y = 77.75i
PRINT x
PRINT y
```

Here are the errors in the code:

1. The variable **"y"** is declared as an **INTEGER**, but the value assigned to it is a floating-point number (**77.75**).

2. The **"i"** suffix after the value **77.75** is not valid in QB64.

To correct these errors, you can update the code as follows:

```
DIM x AS STRING
DIM y AS SINGLE   ' Use SINGLE data type for floating-point numbers
CLS
x = "First Title"
y = 77.75
PRINT x
PRINT y
```

In the corrected code:

- I changed the data type of **"y"** to **SINGLE** to accommodate the floating-point value.
- Removed the **"i"** suffix from the value **77.75**.

Sample Code 7

DIM z AS STRING

DIM x AS INTEGER

DIM y AS INTEGER

DIM a AS INTEGER

CLS

z = "Test"

x = 50

y = 25

a = x + y

PRINT z

PRINT a

This Sample Code does not contain any data type mismatch bug.

CHAPTER 6 - USER INPUT - QB64

In the previous chapters, we focused on hard-coding information directly into the program. However, in this tutorial, we'll explore how to obtain user input. The command used to receive user input is called **INPUT**. When you use **INPUT**, it prompts the user to enter data, which is then stored in a variable. The string prompt and the variable must be separated by either a comma or a semicolon. If you use a semicolon, it will display a question mark at the end of the prompt.

Sample Code 1

```
DIM UserFirstName AS STRING

DIM UserLastName AS STRING

CLS

INPUT "Enter Your First Name: ", UserFirstName

INPUT "Enter Your Last Name: ", UserLastName

PRINT

PRINT "Pleased to make your acquaintance, "; UserFirstName; " "; UserLastName
```

Analysis:

- **DIM**: This statement is used to declare two string variables, UserFirstName and UserLastName.
- **CLS**: Clears the screen before the user inputs their

information.

- **INPUT**: Two input statements collect the user's first and last names and store them in the respective variables.

- **PRINT**: The first print statement adds a blank line for readability.

- **PRINT**: The second print statement outputs a greeting that includes the user's full name.

This code is written in BASIC, which is known for its simplicity and ease of understanding, making it a good choice for beginners. The program prompts the user to enter their first and last names and then greets the user with a personalized message.

Sample Code 2

```
DIM UserFirst AS STRING
DIM UserLast AS STRING
DIM Number1 AS INTEGER
DIM Number2 AS INTEGER

CLS

INPUT "Enter Your First Name: ", UserFirst
INPUT "Enter Your Last Name: ", UserLast

PRINT
PRINT "Pleased to make your acquaintance, "; UserFirst; " ";
UserLast
```

PRINT

INPUT "Enter the First Integer: ", Number1

INPUT "Enter the Second Integer: ", Number2

PRINT

PRINT Number1; " + "; Number2; " = "; Number1 + Number2

Analysis:

- **DIM**: The DIM statements declare four variables: UserFirst, UserLast, Number1, and Number2.
- **CLS**: Clears the screen before input prompts.
- **INPUT**: Collects the user's first name, last name, and two integers.
- **PRINT**: Displays a personalized greeting using the user's full name.
- **PRINT**: Calculates and displays the sum of the two integers.

This code is user-friendly, allowing input for names and numbers, and provides a friendly message. It's a simple example of interactive programming in BASIC.

CHAPTER 7 - IF STATEMENTS - QB64

IF statements are used for conditional branching. They allow you to execute different code blocks based on whether a condition is true or false. Let's break it down:

Syntax:

IF condition THEN

    ' Code to execute if the condition is true

ELSE

    ' Code to execute if the condition is false

END IF

Explanation:

- The condition is an expression that evaluates to either true or false.

- If the condition is true, the code inside the first block (after THEN) is executed.

- If the condition is false, the code inside the second block (after ELSE) is executed (if an ELSE block is provided).

- The END IF statement marks the end of the conditional block.

Example: Let's say we want to check if a user's age is greater than or equal to 18. If it is, we'll print a message saying they are eligible for voting; otherwise, we'll print a different message.

```
DIM UserAge AS INTEGER
INPUT "Enter your age: ", UserAge

IF UserAge >= 18 THEN
    PRINT "You are eligible for voting!"
ELSE
    PRINT "You are not eligible for voting yet."
END IF
```

In this example:

- If the user enters an age of 20, the first message will be printed.
- If the user enters an age of 15, the second message will be printed.

Remember that QB64 supports more complex conditions using logical operators (AND, OR, NOT). You can also nest multiple IF statements to handle various scenarios.

Expression Signs (Relational Operators)

< Less than

<= Less than or equal to

> Greater than

>= Greater than or equal to

= Equal to

<> Not Equal to

If the condition is met, the code associated with condition will trigger.

Sample Code 1

```
CLS
IF 55 > 25 THEN
  PRINT "55 Is Greater Than 25"
END IF
```

Sample Code 2

```
CLS
IF 55 > 100 THEN
  PRINT "55 Is Greater Than 100"
ELSE
  PRINT "55 Is Less Than 100"
END IF
```

Sample Code 3

```
DIM UserInput1 AS INTEGER
DIM UserInput2 AS INTEGER

CLS

INPUT "Enter the First Integer: ", UserInput1
```

INPUT "Enter the Second Integer: ", UserInput2

IF UserInput1 > UserInput2 THEN

    PRINT UserInput1; " is greater than "; UserInput2

ELSEIF UserInput2 > UserInput1 THEN

    PRINT UserInput2; " is greater than "; UserInput1

ELSE

    PRINT "The numbers are the same"

END IF

Analysis:

- **DIM**: We declare two integer variables: UserInput1 and UserInput2.

- **CLS**: Clears the screen before input prompts.

- **INPUT**: Collects the user's input for the first and second integers.

- **IF-ELSEIF-ELSE**: Compares the values of UserInput1 and UserInput2:
    - If UserInput1 is greater, it prints that.
    - If UserInput2 is greater, it prints that.
    - Otherwise, it prints that the numbers are the same.

This code allows the user to input two integers and provides a comparison result.

CHAPTER 8 - SELECT CASE STATEMENTS - QB64

This statement is a powerful tool for handling multiple conditions and making your code more concise. Here's what you need to know:

What is the SELECT CASE statement?

- The **SELECT CASE** statement is similar to **IF** statements, but it allows you to evaluate a single expression against multiple possible values. It simplifies code by avoiding nested **IF-ELSE** structures.

Syntax:

```
SELECT [EVERY] CASE testExpression
    CASE expressionList1
        ' Code block for the first matching value
    CASE expressionList2
        ' Code block for the second matching value
    ' ... (add more CASE blocks as needed)
    CASE ELSE
        ' Code block for when no specific value matches
END SELECT
```

Explanation:

- testExpression is the value you want to compare.
- expressionList1, expressionList2, etc., are the possible values to match against.
- The code block under the matching CASE executes when the value matches.
- The CASE ELSE block runs if no specific value matches.

Example:

```
a = 100
SELECT CASE a
    CASE 1, 3, 5, 7, 9
        PRINT "Odd values under 10 will be shown."
    CASE 10
        PRINT "10 will be shown."
    CASE 50
        PRINT "50 will be shown."
    CASE 100
        PRINT "This will be shown. (a is 100)"
        PRINT "(and this)"
    CASE 150
        PRINT "150 will be shown."
    CASE ELSE
        PRINT "No matching value."
END SELECT
```

In this example:

- If a is 1, 3, 5, 7, or 9, it prints the odd message.

- If a is 10, it prints "10 will be shown."

- If a is 50, it prints "50 will be shown."

- If a is 100, it prints both "This will be shown. (a is 100)" and "(and this)."

- If a is 150 or any other value, it prints "No matching value."

Remember to adapt the values and code blocks according to your specific needs. The **SELECT CASE** statement is a versatile tool for handling different scenarios in your QB64 programs!

Sample Code 1

```
DIM FruitChoice AS STRING

CLS

PRINT "Please choose your favorite fruit:"

PRINT "1. Apple"

PRINT "2. Banana"

PRINT "3. Cherry"

PRINT "4. Date"

INPUT "Enter the number corresponding to your choice: ", FruitChoice

FruitChoice = UCASE$(FruitChoice)

PRINT

SELECT CASE FruitChoice
  CASE "1"
    PRINT "You chose Apple."
```

CASE "2"

PRINT "You chose Banana."

CASE "3"

PRINT "You chose Cherry."

CASE "4"

PRINT "You chose Date."

CASE ELSE

PRINT "Invalid choice, please enter a number from 1 to 4."

END SELECT

Analysis of the Code:

- DIM FruitChoice AS STRING declares a string variable named FruitChoice.

- CLS clears the screen.

- The PRINT statements display a menu of fruits with corresponding numbers.

- INPUT asks the user to enter their choice, which is stored in FruitChoice.

- UCASE$ converts the input to uppercase to ensure consistency, even though it's not necessary in this case since we're dealing with numbers.

- The SELECT CASE statement evaluates FruitChoice.

- Each CASE corresponds to a number that represents a fruit. If FruitChoice matches the number, the corresponding message is printed.

- CASE ELSE provides a default action if the entered value doesn't match any of the specified cases, prompting the user to make a valid choice.

This code is a simple menu system that allows users to select their favorite fruit and provides immediate feedback based on their selection. It demonstrates how the SELECT CASE statement can be used for creating user-friendly interfaces in QB64.

Sample Code 2

```
DIM Temperature AS INTEGER
CLS
PRINT
PRINT "Weather Condition Checker"
INPUT "Enter the current temperature (in Celsius): ", Temperature
PRINT

SELECT CASE Temperature
    CASE IS >= 35
        PRINT "Extreme Heat Warning"
    CASE 30 TO 34
        PRINT "Very Hot"
    CASE 25 TO 29
        PRINT "Hot"
    CASE 20 TO 24
        PRINT "Warm"
    CASE 15 TO 19
        PRINT "Mild"
    CASE 10 TO 14
        PRINT "Cool"
    CASE 5 TO 9
```

```
        PRINT "Cold"
    CASE ELSE
        PRINT "Freezing"
END SELECT
```

Analysis of the Code:

- The original code used test scores to determine grades, while the modified version uses temperature ranges to determine weather conditions.

- The variable Temperature now represents the current temperature in Celsius.

- The SELECT CASE statement evaluates the temperature and prints the corresponding weather condition.

- The CASE ELSE block handles any temperature values that don't fall within the specified ranges.

- This example demonstrates how the SELECT CASE statement can be adapted for different scenarios, making the code more versatile and readable.

Sample Code 3

```
DIM Temperature AS INTEGER
CLS
PRINT
PRINT "Water State Checker"
INPUT "Enter the temperature (in Celsius): ", Temperature
PRINT

SELECT CASE Temperature
```

```
CASE IS <= 0
  PRINT "Solid (Ice)"
CASE 1 TO 99
  PRINT "Liquid (Water)"
CASE IS >= 100
  PRINT "Gas (Steam)"
CASE ELSE
  PRINT "Invalid temperature"
END SELECT
```

Analysis of the Code:

- The original code used test scores to determine grades, while the modified version uses temperature to determine the state of water.

- The variable Temperature now represents the current temperature in Celsius.

- The SELECT CASE statement evaluates the temperature and prints the corresponding state of water.

- The CASE ELSE block handles any temperature values that don't fall within the specified ranges.

- This example demonstrates how the SELECT CASE statement can be adapted for different scenarios, making the code more versatile and readable.

CHAPTER 9 - WHILE LOOP - QB64

In QB64, the WHILE loop is a control flow statement that allows code to be executed repeatedly based on a given Boolean condition. The WHILE loop can be used in two forms: WHILE...WEND and DO...LOOP WHILE.

Here's a basic example of a WHILE loop in QB64:

WHILE condition

   ' Code to execute as long as condition is true

WEND

And here's an example of a DO...LOOP WHILE:

DO

   ' Code to execute

LOOP WHILE condition

In the WHILE...WEND loop, if the condition is False at the beginning, the code inside the loop may not run at all. In contrast, the DO...LOOP WHILE loop will always run at least once because the condition is evaluated at the end of the loop.

Sample Code 1:

DIM count AS INTEGER

CLS

```
count = 5

WHILE count <= 15
  PRINT "FreeCodeCamp"
  count = count + 1
WEND
```

Sample Code 2:

```
DIM num AS INTEGER
CLS
num = 3

WHILE num <> 13
  PRINT "FreeCodeCamp"
  num = num + 2
WEND
```

Sample Code 3:

```
DIM i AS INTEGER
CLS
i = 2

WHILE i <= 12
  PRINT i
  i = i + 2
WEND
```

Sample Code 4:

```
DIM countdown AS INTEGER
CLS
countdown = 20

WHILE countdown > 0
  PRINT countdown
  countdown = countdown - 2
WEND

PRINT
PRINT "LIFTOFF!!!"
```

Sample Code 5:

```
DIM j AS INTEGER
CLS
j = 3

WHILE j <= 21
  PRINT j
  j = j + 3
WEND
```

Sample Code 6:

```
DIM k AS INTEGER
CLS
```

```
k = 4
WHILE k <= 20
  PRINT k
  k = k + 4
WEND
```

Sample Code 7 :

```
DIM n AS INTEGER
CLS
n = 2

WHILE n <= 20
  PRINT n; "Squared ="; n * n
  n = n + 2
WEND
```

CHAPTER 10 - DO LOOP - QB64

In QB64, the DO...LOOP construct is a versatile loop that allows code to repeat based on a given condition. There are two main variations of the DO...LOOP loop: DO WHILE and DO UNTIL.

Here's how they work:

1. **DO WHILE**:
   - The DO WHILE loop executes the code block while a specified condition is true.
   - If the condition is false from the beginning, the code inside the loop may not run at all.
   - Example:
   - DIM counter AS INTEGER
   - counter = 1
   -
   - DO WHILE counter <= 10
   -   PRINT "Hello"
   -   counter = counter + 1
   - LOOP

This code will print "Hello" ten times.

2. **DO UNTIL**:
   - The DO UNTIL loop executes the code block

until a specified condition becomes true.

- If the condition is true from the beginning, the code inside the loop may not run at all.

- Example:

- DIM num AS INTEGER

- num = 1

-

- DO UNTIL num = 11

  - PRINT "Hello"

  - num = num + 1

- LOOP

This code will also print "Hello" ten times.

CHAPTER 11 - FOR LOOP - QB64

The FOR...NEXT loop is a fundamental construct for repeating a block of code a specific number of times. Here's how it works:

Syntax:

FOR counter = startingValue TO endingValue STEP stepSize

' Your loop body code here

NEXT counter

- counter: A numeric variable that keeps track of the loop iteration.

- startingValue: The initial value for the counter.

- endingValue: The final value for the counter. The loop will execute until the counter reaches this value.

- stepSize: The amount by which the counter increments in each iteration. It can be a positive or negative value.

Rules:

- You can use the counter variable within the loop body, but avoid modifying it directly (since it automatically changes).

- Both startingValue and endingValue can be arithmetic expressions or variables.

Example: Let's say we want to print the numbers from 1 to 10:

FOR i = 1 TO 10

      PRINT i

NEXT i

Warning

Ensuring that your loop has a proper termination condition is crucial to prevent infinite loops. When writing loops, consider the following points:

1. **Termination Condition:**
   - Always include a condition that will eventually cause the loop to exit. Without it, the loop will continue indefinitely.
   - For example, in a FOR...NEXT loop, the NEXT statement automatically increments the loop counter and checks if it has reached the specified ending value. If the condition is met, the loop terminates.

2. **CTRL + BREAK:**
   - You're absolutely right! In QB64 (and many other programming environments), pressing CTRL + BREAK can forcefully stop an executing program or infinite loop.
   - It's a handy way to regain control if your code accidentally enters an infinite loop.

Sample Code 1

DIM counter AS INTEGER

CLS

```
FOR counter = 1 TO 10
    PRINT "Lanret Solutions"
NEXT counter
```

- The loop will now iterate from 1 to 10, printing "Lanret Solutions" in each iteration.

Sample Code 2

```
DIM counter AS INTEGER
CLS
FOR counter = 1 TO 10
    PRINT counter
NEXT counter
```

In this code:

- The loop will now iterate from 1 to 10, printing the value of counter in each iteration.

Now, let's analyze the code:

1. **Variable Declaration** (DIM):
   - We declare an integer variable named counter.
   - The DIM statement allocates memory for the variable.

2. **Loop** (FOR...NEXT):
   - The loop starts with counter set to 1 (FOR counter = 1).
   - It continues until counter reaches 10 (TO 10).
   - In each iteration, the value of counter is printed (PRINT counter).

3. **Output**:

1

2

3

4

5

6

7

8

9

10

Sample Code 3

```
DIM counter AS INTEGER
CLS
FOR counter = 20 TO 40
    PRINT counter
NEXT counter
```

In this code:

- The loop will now iterate from 20 to 40, printing the value of counter in each iteration.

Now, let's analyze the code:

1. **Variable Declaration** (DIM):
   - We declare an integer variable named counter.
   - The DIM statement allocates memory for the variable.

2. **Loop** (FOR...NEXT):

- The loop starts with counter set to 20 (FOR counter = 20).

- It continues until counter reaches 40 (TO 40).

- In each iteration, the value of counter is printed (PRINT counter).

3. **Output:**

20

21

22

...

39

40

Sample Code 4

```
DIM counter AS INTEGER
CLS
FOR counter = 20 TO 40 STEP 2
    PRINT counter
NEXT counter
```

In this code:

- The loop will now iterate from 20 to 40 (inclusive), incrementing by 2 in each iteration.

- It will print the value of counter in each step.

Now, let's analyze the code:

1. **Variable Declaration** (DIM):

   - We declare an integer variable named counter.

   - The DIM statement allocates memory for the

variable.

2. **Loop** (FOR...NEXT):

   ◦ The loop starts with counter set to 20 (FOR counter = 20).

   ◦ It continues until counter reaches 40 (TO 40).

   ◦ The STEP 2 specifies that the loop increments by 2 in each iteration.

   ◦ In each iteration, the value of counter is printed (PRINT counter).

3. **Output**:

   20

   22

   24

   ...

   38

   40

Sample Code 5

```
DIM counter AS INTEGER
CLS
FOR counter = 21 TO 40 STEP 2
    PRINT counter
NEXT counter
```

In this revised code:

   · The loop will now iterate from 21 to 40 (inclusive), incrementing by 2 in each iteration.

   · It will print the value of counter in each step.

Now, let's analyze the code:

1. **Variable Declaration** (DIM):

    ◦ We declare an integer variable named counter.

    ◦ The DIM statement allocates memory for the variable.

2. **Loop** (FOR...NEXT):

    ◦ The loop starts with counter set to 21 (FOR counter = 21).

    ◦ It continues until counter reaches 40 (TO 40).

    ◦ The STEP 2 specifies that the loop increments by 2 in each iteration.

    ◦ In each iteration, the value of counter is printed (PRINT counter).

3. **Output**:

    21

    23

    25

    ...

    39

Sample Code 6

```
DIM x AS INTEGER
CLS
FOR x = 10 TO 1 STEP -1
    PRINT x
NEXT x
```

Here's what this code does:

1. **Variable Declaration** (DIM):

- We declare an integer variable named x.

- The DIM statement allocates memory for the variable.

2. **Clear Screen** (CLS):
    - The CLS command clears the screen, ensuring a clean output area.

3. **Loop** (FOR...NEXT):
    - The loop starts with x set to 10 (FOR x = 10).

    - It continues until x reaches 1 (TO 1).

    - The STEP -1 specifies that the loop decrements by 1 in each iteration.

    - In each iteration, the value of x is printed (PRINT x).

4. **Output**:

    10

    9

    8

    7

    6

    5

    4

    3

    2

    1

CHAPTER 12 – CREATING A SIMPLE CALCULATOR PROGRAM WITH INPUT VALIDATION

- QB64

In this tutorial, we'll build a basic calculator program that interacts with the user.

The program will:

1. Ask the user to input two numbers.

2. Prompt the user to choose an operation (addition, subtraction, multiplication, or division).

3. Perform the selected operation on the two numbers.

4. Display the result.

5. Ask the user if they want to repeat the program or quit.

Additionally, we'll implement input validation to ensure that the user enters valid numeric data.

Step-by-Step Implementation

1. **User Input:**

- The program will ask the user to input two numbers (let's call them num1 and num2).

2. **Operation Selection**:
   - The user will choose an operation (addition, subtraction, multiplication, or division).
   - We'll validate the user's choice to ensure it's a valid operation.

3. **Perform Calculation**:
   - Based on the selected operation, the program will perform the corresponding calculation:
     - Addition: result = num1 + num2
     - Subtraction: result = num1 - num2
     - Multiplication: result = num1 * num2
     - Division: result = num1 / num2

4. **Display Result**:
   - The program will display the calculated result to the user.

5. **Repeat or Quit**:
   - After displaying the result, the program will ask the user if they want to repeat the calculation or quit.
   - If the user chooses to repeat, the process will start again.
   - If the user chooses to quit, the program will exit.

6. **Input Validation**:
   - We'll validate user input to ensure that:
     - The entered values are numeric.
     - The operation choice is valid (addition, subtraction, multiplication, or division).

Example Interaction

Welcome to the Simple Calculator!

Enter the first number: 10

Enter the second number: 5

Choose an operation:

1. Add

2. Subtract

3. Multiply

4. Divide

Enter your choice (1/2/3/4): 3

Result: 10 * 5 = 50

Do you want to calculate again? (yes/no): yes

Enter the first number: 15

Enter the second number: 3

Choose an operation:

1. Add

2. Subtract

3. Multiply

4. Divide

Enter your choice (1/2/3/4): 2

Result: 15 - 3 = 12

Do you want to calculate again? (yes/no): no

Thank you for using the Simple Calculator!

Sample Code 1

Sample Code 1

```
' Simple Calculator Program with Input Validation

Dim num1 As Double
Dim num2 As Double
Dim operation As String
Dim result As Double
Dim repeat As String

CLS
Print "Welcome to the Simple Calculator!"

Do
    ' Get user input for two numbers
    Input "Enter the first number: "; num1
    Input "Enter the second number: "; num2

    ' Get user input for the operation
    Print "Choose an operation:"
```

```
Print "1. Add"
Print "2. Subtract"
Print "3. Multiply"
Print "4. Divide"
Input "Enter your choice (1/2/3/4): "; operation

' Perform the selected operation
Select Case operation
    Case "1"
        result = num1 + num2
    Case "2"
        result = num1 - num2
    Case "3"
        result = num1 * num2
    Case "4"
        If num2 <> 0 Then
            result = num1 / num2
        Else
            Print "Error: Division by zero!"
            End
        End If
    Case Else
        Print "Invalid operation choice!"
        End
End Select
' Display the result
```

```
    Print "Result:", num1, operation, num2, "=", result

    ' Ask if the user wants to repeat or quit
    Input "Do you want to calculate again? (yes/no): "; repeat
    CLS
Loop Until repeat <> "yes"

Print "Thank you for using the Simple Calculator!"
```

CHAPTER 13 - RANDOM NUMBERS - QB64

In QB64 (and its predecessor, QBasic), you can use the RND function to generate random numbers. Here are some key points about using RND:

1. **RND Function:**
   - The RND function generates pseudo-random numbers.
   - The random numbers generated by RND range from 0 (inclusive) to 0.9999999 (exclusive) as **SINGLE** values.
   - The value never equals exactly 1.
   - To get values in a larger range, you can multiply the result of RND by a scaling factor.
   - To start at a specific minimum value, add that number to the RND result (since RND minimums can be 0).

2. **Example Usage:**

3. CLS

4. RANDOMIZE TIMER ' Initialize random seed based on system time

5. Num1 = INT(RND * 100) + 1 ' Generate a random integer

between 1 and 100

6. PRINT "Random Number between 1 and 100:", Num1

7. END

In this example:

- RANDOMIZE TIMER initializes the random seed based on the system time.

- INT(RND * 100) + 1 generates a random integer between 1 and 100.

8. **Pitfalls and Considerations:**
    - Be aware of the limitations of pseudo-randomness. The illusion of randomness in computers is achieved through complex algorithms with input from system clocks.

    - If you need truly random numbers (e.g., for cryptographic purposes), consider using external hardware or specialized libraries.

Remember that while RND provides a convenient way to generate random numbers, it's not suitable for all scenarios. For critical applications, explore other methods or libraries that offer better randomness.

Sample Code 1

```
DIM x AS INTEGER
CLS
FOR x = 1 TO 50
  RANDOMIZE TIMER
  PRINT (RND * 80);
NEXT x
```

1. DIM x AS INTEGER:
    - This line declares an integer variable named x.
    - The DIM statement is used to declare variables in QB64 (and QBasic).
    - In this case, x is declared as an integer.

2. CLS:
    - The CLS command clears the screen (console) by removing any previously displayed text.
    - It ensures that the output starts from a clean slate.

3. FOR x = 1 TO 50:
    - This line starts a loop that iterates from 1 to 50 (inclusive).
    - The loop variable is x.

4. RANDOMIZE TIMER:
    - The RANDOMIZE TIMER statement initializes the random number generator with the current system time.
    - This ensures that subsequent calls to RND produce different random values during each program run.

5. PRINT (RND * 80);:
    - The PRINT statement displays the result of the expression (RND * 80) on the screen.
    - RND generates a random number between 0 (inclusive) and 0.9999999 (exclusive).
    - Multiplying by 80 scales this range to 0 to 79.9999992.
    - The semicolon (;) at the end of the PRINT statement suppresses the newline,

so the next value will be printed on the same line.

6. NEXT x:

- The NEXT statement marks the end of the loop.

- It increments the loop variable (x) and continues the loop until x reaches 50.

Summary:

- The code generates 50 random numbers between 0 and 79.9999992 (inclusive) and prints them on the same line.

- The actual output will be a sequence of decimal numbers (e.g., 12.3456789 56.7890123 ...).

Sample Code 2

```
DIM x AS INTEGER
CLS
FOR x = 1 TO 50
   RANDOMIZE TIMER
   PRINT INT(RND * 30);
NEXT x
```

1. DIM x AS INTEGER:

- This line declares an integer variable named x.

- The DIM statement is used to declare variables in QB64 (and QBasic).

- In this case, x is declared as an integer.

2. CLS:

- The CLS command clears the screen (console) by removing any previously displayed text.

- It ensures that the output starts from a clean slate.

3. FOR x = 1 TO 50:
   - This line starts a loop that iterates from 1 to 50 (inclusive).
   - The loop variable is x.

4. RANDOMIZE TIMER:
   - The RANDOMIZE TIMER statement initializes the random number generator with the current system time.
   - This ensures that subsequent calls to RND produce different random values during each program run.

5. PRINT INT(RND * 30);:
   - The PRINT statement displays the result of the expression INT(RND * 30) on the screen.
   - RND generates a random number between 0 (inclusive) and 0.9999999 (exclusive).
   - Multiplying by 30 scales this range to 0 to 29.999997 (inclusive).
   - The INT function truncates the decimal part, resulting in integers from 0 to 29.
   - The semicolon (;) at the end of the PRINT statement suppresses the newline, so the next value will be printed on the same line.

6. NEXT x:
   - The NEXT statement marks the end of the loop.
   - It increments the loop variable (x) and continues the loop until x reaches 50.

Summary:

- The code generates 50 random integers between 0 and 29 (inclusive) and prints them on the same line.

- The actual output will be a sequence of integers (e.g., 5 12 0 23 ...).

Sample Code 3

```
DIM x AS INTEGER
CLS
FOR x = 1 TO 50
  RANDOMIZE TIMER
  PRINT INT(RND * 20) + 1;
NEXT x
```

1. DIM x AS INTEGER:
     - This line declares an integer variable named x.
     - The DIM statement is used to declare variables in QB64 (and QBasic).
     - In this case, x is declared as an integer.
2. CLS:
     - The CLS command clears the screen (console) by removing any previously displayed text.
     - It ensures that the output starts from a clean slate.
3. FOR x = 1 TO 50:
     - This line starts a loop that iterates from 1 to 50 (inclusive).
     - The loop variable is x.
4. RANDOMIZE TIMER:

- The RANDOMIZE TIMER statement initializes the random number generator with the current system time.

- This ensures that subsequent calls to RND produce different random values during each program run.

5. PRINT INT(RND * 30);:

- The PRINT statement displays the result of the expression INT(RND * 30) on the screen.

- RND generates a random number between 0 (inclusive) and 0.9999999 (exclusive).

- Multiplying by 30 scales this range to 0 to 29.999997 (inclusive).

- The INT function truncates the decimal part, resulting in integers from 0 to 29.

- The semicolon (;) at the end of the PRINT statement suppresses the newline, so the next value will be printed on the same line.

6. NEXT x:

- The NEXT statement marks the end of the loop.

- It increments the loop variable (x) and continues the loop until x reaches 50.

Summary:

- The code generates 50 random integers between 0 and 29 (inclusive) and prints them on the same line.

- The actual output will be a sequence of integers (e.g., 5 12 0 23 ...).

Sample Code 4

```
DIM x AS INTEGER
CLS
FOR x = 1 TO 10
  PRINT INT(RND * 20) + 1;
NEXT x
```

1. DIM x AS INTEGER:
   - This line declares an integer variable named x.
   - The DIM statement is used to declare variables in QB64 (and QBasic).
   - In this case, x is declared as an integer.

2. CLS:
   - The CLS command clears the screen (console) by removing any previously displayed text.
   - It ensures that the output starts from a clean slate.

3. FOR x = 1 TO 10:
   - This line starts a loop that iterates from 1 to 10 (inclusive).
   - The loop variable is x.

4. PRINT INT(RND * 20) + 1;:
   - The PRINT statement displays the result of the expression INT(RND * 20) + 1 on the screen.
   - RND generates a random number between 0 (inclusive) and 0.9999999 (exclusive).
   - Multiplying by 20 scales this range to 0 to 19.9999998.
   - The INT function truncates the decimal part, resulting in integers from 0 to 19.

- Adding 1 ensures that the final result is between 1 and 20 (inclusive).

- The semicolon (;) at the end of the PRINT statement suppresses the newline, so the next value will be printed on the same line.

5. NEXT x:

- The NEXT statement marks the end of the loop.

- It increments the loop variable (x) and continues the loop until x reaches 10.

Summary:

- The code generates 10 random integers between 1 and 20 (inclusive) and prints them on the same line.

- The actual output will be a sequence of integers (e.g., 5 12 20 3 ...).

Sample Code 5

```
DIM x AS INTEGER
DIM RNum AS INTEGER
CLS
FOR x = 1 TO 50
  RANDOMIZE TIMER
  RNum = (RND * 50) + 1
  PRINT RNum;
NEXT x
```

1. DIM x AS INTEGER and DIM RNum AS INTEGER:

- These lines declare two integer variables: x and RNum.

- The DIM statement is used to declare variables in QB64 (and QBasic).

- Both x and RNum are declared as integers.

2. CLS:

- The CLS command clears the screen (console) by removing any previously displayed text.

- It ensures that the output starts from a clean slate.

3. FOR x = 1 TO 50:

- This line starts a loop that iterates from 1 to 50 (inclusive).

- The loop variable is x.

4. RANDOMIZE TIMER:

- The RANDOMIZE TIMER statement initializes the random number generator with the current system time.

- This ensures that subsequent calls to RND produce different random values during each program run.

5. RNum = (RND * 50) + 1:

- This line generates a random number between 1 and 50 (inclusive) and assigns it to the variable RNum.

- RND generates a random number between 0 (inclusive) and 0.9999999 (exclusive).

- Multiplying by 50 scales this range to 0 to 49.9999995.

- Adding 1 ensures that the final result is between 1 and 50 (inclusive).

6. PRINT RNum;:

- The PRINT statement displays the value of

RNum on the screen.

- The semicolon (;) at the end of the PRINT statement suppresses the newline, so the next value will be printed on the same line.

7. NEXT x:

- The NEXT statement marks the end of the loop.

- It increments the loop variable (x) and continues the loop until x reaches 50.

Summary:

- The code generates 50 random integers between 1 and 50 (inclusive) and prints them on the same line.

- The actual output will be a sequence of integers (e.g., 5 12 20 3 ...).

Sample Code 6

```
DIM x AS INTEGER
DIM RNum AS INTEGER
CLS
FOR x = 1 TO 50
  RANDOMIZE TIMER
  RNum = (RND * 20)
  PRINT RNum;
NEXT x
```

1. DIM x AS INTEGER and DIM RNum AS INTEGER:
   - These lines declare two integer variables: x and RNum.
   - The DIM statement is used to declare variables

in QB64 (and QBasic).

 ◦ Both x and RNum are declared as integers.

2. CLS:

 ◦ The CLS command clears the screen (console) by removing any previously displayed text.

 ◦ It ensures that the output starts from a clean slate.

3. FOR x = 1 TO 50:

 ◦ This line starts a loop that iterates from 1 to 50 (inclusive).

 ◦ The loop variable is x.

4. RANDOMIZE TIMER:

 ◦ The RANDOMIZE TIMER statement initializes the random number generator with the current system time.

 ◦ This ensures that subsequent calls to RND produce different random values during each program run.

5. RNum = (RND * 20):

 ◦ This line generates a random number between 0 (inclusive) and 0.9999999 (exclusive) using RND.

 ◦ Multiplying by 20 scales this range to 0 to 19.9999998.

 ◦ However, the result is still a floating-point value.

 ◦ Since RNum is declared as an integer, the decimal part is truncated, resulting in integers from 0 to 19.

6. PRINT RNum;:

 ◦ The PRINT statement displays the value of

RNum on the screen.

- The semicolon (;) at the end of the PRINT statement suppresses the newline, so the next value will be printed on the same line.

7. NEXT x:

- The NEXT statement marks the end of the loop.
- It increments the loop variable (x) and continues the loop until x reaches 50.

Summary:

- The code generates 50 random integers between 0 and 19 (inclusive) and prints them on the same line.
- The actual output will be a sequence of integers (e.g., 5 12 20 3 ...).

Sample Code 7

```
DIM x AS INTEGER
DIM RNum AS INTEGER
CLS
FOR x = 1 TO 50
  RANDOMIZE TIMER
  RNum = (RND * 7) + 1
  PRINT RNum;
NEXT x
```

1. DIM x AS INTEGER and DIM RNum AS INTEGER:
   - These lines declare two integer variables: x and RNum.
   - The DIM statement is used to declare variables

in QB64 (and QBasic).

- Both x and RNum are declared as integers.

2. CLS:

- The CLS command clears the screen (console) by removing any previously displayed text.

- It ensures that the output starts from a clean slate.

3. FOR x = 1 TO 50:

- This line starts a loop that iterates from 1 to 50 (inclusive).

- The loop variable is x.

4. RANDOMIZE TIMER:

- The RANDOMIZE TIMER statement initializes the random number generator with the current system time.

- This ensures that subsequent calls to RND produce different random values during each program run.

5. RNum = (RND * 7) + 1:

- This line generates a random number between 0 (inclusive) and 0.9999999 (exclusive) using RND.

- Multiplying by 7 scales this range to 0 to 6.9999993.

- Adding 1 ensures that the final result is between 1 and 7 (inclusive).

6. PRINT RNum;:

- The PRINT statement displays the value of RNum on the screen.

- The semicolon (;) at the end of the PRINT statement suppresses the newline, so the next value will be printed on the same line.

7. NEXT x:

- The NEXT statement marks the end of the loop.

- It increments the loop variable (x) and continues the loop until x reaches 50.

Summary:

- The code generates 50 random integers between 1 and 7 (inclusive) and prints them on the same line.

- The actual output will be a sequence of integers (e.g., 5 3 7 2 …).

CHAPTER 14 - ARRAYS - QB64

In QB64, an array is a collection of values stored in a single variable. Arrays can hold lists of variables of the same data type. When there are large lists of variables and data, it is easier to contain the data in an array than have large amounts of separate variables to hold the data.

The syntax to declare an array in QB64 is as follows:

DIM array_name (number_of_items) AS datatype

For example, to declare an array of 10 integers, you would write:

DIM myArray(10) AS INTEGER

You can also have multidimensional arrays. For example, a two-dimensional array can be declared as follows:

DIM my2DArray(10, 10) AS INTEGER

Sample Code 1

```
DIM i AS INTEGER

CLS

NamesArray(1) = "Joe"

NamesArray(2) = "Jim"

NamesArray(3) = "Jill"

NamesArray(4) = "Joan"

NamesArray(5) = "Jan"
```

```
FOR i = 1 TO 5

   PRINT NamesArray(i)

NEXT i
```

1. DIM i AS INTEGER: This line declares a variable i as an integer. This variable will be used as a counter in the loop that follows.

2. CLS: This command clears the screen. It's often used at the beginning of programs to ensure that the output starts on a clean screen.

3. NamesArray(1) = "Joe" to NamesArray(5) = "Jan": These lines assign string values to the elements of the NamesArray array. The array is indexed from 1 to 5, and each index corresponds to a different name.

4. FOR i = 1 TO 5: This line starts a FOR loop that will iterate over the elements of the NamesArray array. The variable i will take on the values 1 through 5, inclusive.

5. PRINT NamesArray(i): Inside the loop, this line prints the value of the NamesArray element at the current index i. As i changes with each iteration of the loop, a different name will be printed each time.

6. NEXT i: This line marks the end of the FOR loop. After this line is executed, the program will loop back to the FOR statement, and i will be incremented by 1. When i exceeds 5, the loop will terminate.

So, in summary, this program will print the names "Joe", "Jim", "Jill", "Joan", and "Jan" on separate lines on the screen. Each name corresponds to an element in the NamesArray array. The names are printed in the order they are assigned in the array

Sample Code 2

```
DIM Numbers(5) AS INTEGER
DIM counter AS INTEGER
DIM Total AS INTEGER
CLS
Numbers(1) = 15
Numbers(2) = 20
Numbers(3) = 5
Numbers(4) = 10
Numbers(5) = 10
Total = 0
FOR counter = 1 TO 5
    Total = Total + Numbers(counter)
NEXT counter
PRINT "The Sum Is:"; Total
```

1. DIM Numbers(5) AS INTEGER: This line declares an array named Numbers with 5 elements, each of which is an integer.

2. DIM counter AS INTEGER: This line declares a variable counter as an integer. This variable will be used as a counter in the loop that follows.

3. DIM Total AS INTEGER: This line declares a variable Total as an integer. This variable will be used to store the sum of the elements in the Numbers array.

4. CLS: This command clears the screen. It's often used at the beginning of programs to ensure that the output starts on a clean screen.

5. Numbers(1) = 15 to Numbers(5) = 10: These lines assign

integer values to the elements of the Numbers array. The array is indexed from 1 to 5, and each index corresponds to a different number.

6. Total = 0: This line initializes the Total variable to 0. This is necessary because Total will be used to store the sum of the elements in the Numbers array, and it needs to start from 0.

7. FOR counter = 1 TO 5: This line starts a FOR loop that will iterate over the elements of the Numbers array. The variable counter will take on the values 1 through 5, inclusive.

8. Total = Total + Numbers(counter): Inside the loop, this line adds the value of the Numbers element at the current index counter to the Total. As counter changes with each iteration of the loop, a different number will be added to Total each time.

9. NEXT counter: This line marks the end of the FOR loop. After this line is executed, the program will loop back to the FOR statement, and counter will be incremented by 1. When counter exceeds 5, the loop will terminate.

10. PRINT "The Sum Is:"; Total: This line prints the string "The Sum Is:" followed by the value of Total, which is the sum of the elements in the Numbers array.

So, in summary, this program will calculate the sum of the numbers 15, 20, 5, 10, and 10, and then print "The Sum Is:" followed by the sum. The screen is cleared before the calculation and printing to ensure they start on a clean screen. The FOR loop is used to iterate over the elements of the Numbers array and add each one to Total. The PRINT statement prints the string "The Sum Is:" followed by the sum.

CHAPTER 15 - PARALLEL ARRAYS - QB64

Parallel arrays, also known as **structure-of-arrays (SoA)**, are a fundamental concept in programming. Let me explain what they are and how they work.

1. **Definition of Parallel Arrays**:
    - Parallel arrays consist of **multiple arrays of the same size**. Each element in these arrays is closely related, and together, they represent an object or entity.

    - For example, consider two parallel arrays: one representing the x-coordinates and the other representing the y-coordinates of n points. The i-th element in each array corresponds to the same point's coordinates.

2. **Working with Parallel Arrays**:
    - Parallel arrays allow you to store different types of data related to a single record.

    - Common use cases include storing data for students (e.g., roll number, marks, result) or weather forecasts (e.g., temperature, humidity, wind speed).

    - The key requirement is that the arrays must have the **same number of elements**, and the data must line up from array to array.

3. **Advantages and Disadvantages**:
   ◦ **Advantages**:
     ▪ **Simplicity**: Parallel arrays are straightforward to understand and implement.
     ▪ **Speed**: Accessing elements in parallel arrays is efficient because they are contiguous in memory.
     ▪ **Locality of Reference**: Data related to the same entity is stored close together, improving cache performance.

   ◦ **Disadvantages**:
     ▪ **Cost of Growing or Shrinking**: If you need to add or remove elements, resizing parallel arrays can be cumbersome.
     ▪ **Maintenance**: Ensuring consistency across parallel arrays requires careful handling.

4. **Example**:
   ◦ Suppose we have three students:
     ▪ Student 1: Roll number 101, marks 85, result "Pass"
     ▪ Student 2: Roll number 102, marks 92, result "Pass"
     ▪ Student 3: Roll number 103, marks 78, result "Fail"
   ◦ We can use parallel arrays as follows:
     ▪ rollNumbers = [101, 102, 103]
     ▪ marks = [85, 92, 78]
     ▪ results = ["Pass", "Pass", "Fail"]

5. **QB64 and Parallel Arrays**:
   ◦ QB64 is a modern version of QBasic, and it supports parallel arrays.

Sample Code 1

Let's create a simple QB64 program that uses parallel arrays to store student information. We'll use the provided data for rollNumbers, marks, and results.

Here's an example program:

```
' QB64 Program: Student Information Using Parallel Arrays
DIM SHARED rollNumbers(2) AS INTEGER
DIM SHARED marks(2) AS INTEGER
DIM SHARED results(2) AS STRING

' Initialize the parallel arrays
rollNumbers(0) = 101
rollNumbers(1) = 102
rollNumbers(2) = 103

marks(0) = 85
marks(1) = 92
marks(2) = 78

results(0) = "Pass"
results(1) = "Pass"
results(2) = "Fail"

' Display student information
PRINT "Student Information:"
FOR i = 0 TO 2
```

```
        PRINT "Roll Number: "; rollNumbers(i)

        PRINT "Marks: "; marks(i)

        PRINT "Result: "; results(i)

        PRINT

NEXT i


' Example: Accessing specific student's data

studentIndex = 1 ' Change this to access a different student (0, 1, or
2)

PRINT "Student ", rollNumbers(studentIndex)

PRINT "Marks: ", marks(studentIndex)

PRINT "Result: ", results(studentIndex)


END
```

' Note: You can modify the data in the parallel arrays as needed.

In this program:

- We declare three parallel arrays: rollNumbers, marks, and results.

- Each array corresponds to a specific aspect of student information.

- The FOR loop iterates through the arrays to display all student data.

- You can change the studentIndex variable to access information for a specific student (0, 1, or 2).

CHAPTER 16 - 2 DIMENSIONAL ARRAY - MATRIX - QB64

A **two-dimensional array** (often referred to as a **matrix**) is an array that has two dimensions: rows and columns. It's like a grid where each cell can hold a value. In QB64, you can create a 2D array using the DIM statement.

Here's an example of how to declare a 2D integer array in QB64:

DIM myMatrix(3, 3) AS INTEGER

In this example:

- myMatrix is the name of the array.

- The first parameter (3) represents the number of rows.

- The second parameter (3) represents the number of columns.

Think of matrices as arrays that contain arrays as elements. For instance, you could use a 2D array to represent a chessboard, a grid, or even a deck of cards. Speaking of which, let's create a 2D array for a deck of cards:

1. **Suits** (4 in total): **Diamonds, Spades, Hearts, Clubs**

2. **Ranks** (13 in total): **2, 3, 4, 5, 6, 7, 8, 9, 10, Jack, Queen, King, Ace**

We can create a 2D array by combining the array of suits and the array of ranks. Each cell will represent a specific card (e.g., "Ace of

Spades").

Sample Code 1

```
DIM matrix(5, 5) AS INTEGER

' Fill the matrix with values
FOR i = 1 TO 5
    FOR j = 1 TO 5
        matrix(i, j) = i * j
    NEXT j
NEXT i

' Print the matrix
FOR i = 1 TO 5
    FOR j = 1 TO 5
        PRINT matrix(i, j);
    NEXT j
    PRINT
NEXT i
```

In this code:

- DIM matrix(5, 5) AS INTEGER declares a two-dimensional array named matrix with 5 rows and 5 columns.

- The nested FOR loops are used to fill the matrix with the product of the current row and column indices.

- The second set of nested FOR loops prints out each element in the matrix, formatting it as a 5x5 grid.

You can modify the size of the matrix and the values you assign to each element to suit your needs.

CHAPTER 17 - READ AND DATA MATRIX - QB64

In QB64, the READ and DATA statements are used to read data from a data file (usually included in the program) into an array. Let's create a simple program that reads data from a matrix stored in the DATA statements and prints it out.

DIM matrix(5, 5) AS INTEGER

```
' Read data from DATA statements and populate the matrix
FOR i = 1 TO 5
    FOR j = 1 TO 5
        READ matrix(i, j)
    NEXT j
NEXT i


' Print the matrix
FOR i = 1 TO 5
    FOR j = 1 TO 5
        PRINT matrix(i, j);
    NEXT j
    PRINT
```

NEXT i

DATA 10, 20, 30, 40, 50

DATA 60, 70, 80, 90, 100

DATA 110, 120, 130, 140, 150

DATA 160, 170, 180, 190, 200

DATA 210, 220, 230, 240, 250

In this program:

- We declare a two-dimensional array named matrix with 5 rows and 5 columns.

- The READ statement reads data from the DATA statements and populates the matrix.

- The PRINT statements display the matrix on the screen.

CHAPTER 18 - PREVENTING DUPLICATE DATA IN THE SAME ARRAY - QB64

Preventing duplicate data in an array is essential to maintain data integrity and avoid redundancy. In QB64, you can achieve this by checking the contents of the array before adding new data. Let's explore a simple example using an array of first names:

Sample Code 1

```
Dim row As Integer

Dim FirstNames(100) As String

Dim newName As String


' Initialize the array with some existing names (for demonstration purposes)

FirstNames(1) = "Alice"

FirstNames(2) = "Bob"

FirstNames(3) = "Charlie"
```

```
' Prompt the user for a new name
Input "Enter a first name: ", newName

' Check if the name already exists in the array
For row = 1 To 100
    If FirstNames(row) = newName Then
        Print "Name already exists. Please enter another name."
        End
    End If
Next row

' Add the new name to the array
For row = 1 To 100
    If FirstNames(row) = "" Then
        FirstNames(row) = newName
        Exit For
    End If
Next row

' Display the updated array
For row = 1 To 100
    If FirstNames(row) <> "" Then
        Print FirstNames(row);
    End If
Next row
```

In this program:

1. We initialize an array called FirstNames with some existing names.

2. The user enters a new name (newName).

3. We check if the name already exists in the array. If it does, we prompt the user for another name.

4. If the name is not found, we add it to the first available slot in the array.

5. Finally, we display the updated array without duplicates.

CHAPTER 19 - STRING MANIPULATION - QB64

Let's explore string manipulation in QB64. String manipulation involves various operations on strings, such as concatenation, extraction, and modification. I'll provide an example of how to manipulate strings in QB64.

First, let's consider concatenation. You can combine strings using the + operator. Here's a simple program that demonstrates string concatenation:

DIM firstName AS STRING

DIM lastName AS STRING

DIM fullName AS STRING

firstName = "John"

lastName = "Doe"

fullName = firstName + " " + lastName

PRINT "Full Name: "; fullName

In this program:

- We declare three string variables: firstName, lastName, and fullName.

- We assign values to firstName and lastName.

- The + operator concatenates the first name, a space, and the last name to form the full name.

- Finally, we print the full name.

Next, let's explore other string manipulation techniques, such as extracting substrings, converting case (uppercase/lowercase), and searching for specific patterns within strings.

Extracting Substrings: You can extract a portion of a string using the MID$ function. It allows you to specify the starting position and the length of the substring. Here's an example:

DIM myString AS STRING

myString = "Hello, World!"

' Extract the substring starting from position 8 (W) with a length of 5 characters

PRINT MID$(myString, 8, 5) ' Output: "World"

Converting Case: QB64 provides functions to convert strings to uppercase (UCASE$) and lowercase (LCASE$). Here's how you can use them:

DIM originalString AS STRING

originalString = "Hello, QB64!"

PRINT UCASE$(originalString) ' Output: "HELLO, QB64!"

PRINT LCASE$(originalString) ' Output: "hello, qb64!"

Searching for Patterns: You can search for specific substrings within a larger string using the INSTR function. It returns the position of the first occurrence of the specified substring. If not found, it returns 0.

```
DIM searchIn AS STRING
searchIn = "The quick brown fox jumps over the lazy dog."

' Search for the word "fox"
PRINT INSTR(searchIn, "fox") ' Output: 17 (position of "f" in "fox")
PRINT INSTR(searchIn, "cat") ' Output: 0 (not found)
```

Sample Code

```
CLS
PRINT LEN("QB64")
```

Let's analyze the given code snippet:

```
PRINT LEN("QB64")
```

1. The LEN function in QB64 returns the length (number of characters) of a given string.
2. In this case, the string being evaluated is "QB64".
3. The LEN("QB64") expression calculates the length of the string "QB64" and prints the result.

The output of this code will be the length of the string "QB64", which is **4** characters.

Sample Code

```
CLS
PRINT MID$("QB64", 1, 1)
```

Let's analyze the given code snippet:

PRINT MID$("QB64", 1, 1)

1. The MID$ function in QB64 extracts a substring from a given string.

2. In this case, the string being evaluated is "QB64".

3. The first parameter (1) specifies the starting position (index) within the string.

4. The second parameter (1) specifies the length of the substring to extract.

5. Therefore, MID$("QB64", 1, 1) extracts a substring starting from the first character (index 1) with a length of 1 character.

6. The result of this expression is the first character of the string, which is **"Q"**.

When you run this code, it will print the letter "Q" to the console.

Sample Code

CLS

PRINT MID$("QB64", 1, 2)

Let's analyze the given code snippet:

PRINT MID$("QB64", 1, 2)

1. The MID$ function in QB64 extracts a substring from a given string.

2. In this case, the string being evaluated is "QB64".

3. The first parameter (1) specifies the starting position (index) within the string.

4. The second parameter (2) specifies the length of the substring to extract.

5. Therefore, MID$("QB64", 1, 2) extracts a substring starting from the first character (index 1) with a length of 2 characters.

6. The result of this expression is the first two characters of the string, which are **"QB"**.

When you run this code, it will print the letters "QB" to the console.

Sample Code

CLS

PRINT MID$("School", 4, 2)

Let's analyze the given code snippet:

PRINT MID$("School", 4, 2)

1. The MID$ function in QB64 extracts a substring from a given string.

2. In this case, the string being evaluated is "School".

3. The first parameter (4) specifies the starting position (index) within the string.

4. The second parameter (2) specifies the length of the substring to extract.

5. Therefore, MID$("School", 4, 2) extracts a substring starting from the fourth character (index 4) with a length of 2 characters.

6. The result of this expression is the substring "ho".

When you run this code, it will print the letters "ho" to the console.

Sample Code

CLS

LOCATE 14, 22

PRINT "Transformation"

Let's analyze the provided code snippet:

LOCATE 14, 22

PRINT "Transformation"

1. The LOCATE statement in QB64 is used to position the cursor (text cursor) on the screen at a specific row and column.

2. In this case:
   - The first parameter (14) specifies the row number (vertical position).
   - The second parameter (22) specifies the column number (horizontal position).
   - Therefore, LOCATE 14, 22 positions the cursor at row 14 and column 22 on the screen.

3. After positioning the cursor, the PRINT statement is used to display the string "Transformation" at that location.

When you run this code, it will place the text "Transformation" on the screen starting from row 14, column 22.

CHAPTER 19 - PALINDROME PROGRAM - QB64

Let's create a simple **palindrome program** in QB64. A palindrome is a word, phrase, or number that reads the same backward as forward. For example, "madam," "racecar," and "10801" are palindromes.

Here's a QB64 program that checks if a given word (string) is a palindrome:

```
DIM word AS STRING

DIM reversedWord AS STRING

DIM i AS INTEGER


CLS
INPUT "Enter a word: ", word


' Reverse the word
FOR i = LEN(word) TO 1 STEP -1
    reversedWord = reversedWord + MID$(word, i, 1)
NEXT i


' Compare the original word with the reversed word
```

```
IF LCASE$(word) = LCASE$(reversedWord) THEN
    PRINT word; " is a palindrome."
ELSE
    PRINT word; " is not a palindrome."
END IF

END
```

In this program:

1. We input a word from the user.

2. We reverse the word by extracting each character from the end.

3. We compare the original word (converted to lowercase) with the reversed word (also converted to lowercase).

4. If they match, we print that the word is a palindrome; otherwise, we print that it's not.

CHAPTER 20 - ASCII PROGRAM - SEPARATING LETTERS, NUMBERS, AND OTHER CHARACTERS - QB64

Let's create a program in QB64 that separates letters, numbers, and other characters from a given string using ASCII codes. This will help us categorize each character based on its ASCII value.

```
DIM inputString AS STRING

DIM i AS INTEGER

DIM charCode AS INTEGER


CLS
INPUT "Enter a string: ", inputString


FOR i = 1 TO LEN(inputString)

    charCode = ASC(MID$(inputString, i, 1))
```

```
IF (charCode >= 65 AND charCode <= 90) OR (charCode >= 97
AND charCode <= 122) THEN
    PRINT MID$(inputString, i, 1) + " is a letter."
ELSEIF charCode >= 48 AND charCode <= 57 THEN
    PRINT MID$(inputString, i, 1) + " is a number."
ELSE
    PRINT MID$(inputString, i, 1) + " is another character."
END IF
NEXT i


END
```

In this program:

- We input a string from the user.
- For each character in the string:
    - We calculate its ASCII code using ASC.
    - If the code falls within the range of uppercase or lowercase letters, we classify it as a letter.
    - If the code represents a digit (0-9), we classify it as a number.
    - Otherwise, we consider it as another character.

CHAPTER 21 - SOUND AND MUSIC - QB64

QB64 is a modern extended BASIC programming language that sound and music in its source code.

Here are some ways to work with sound and music in QB64:

1. **BEEP Command:**
   - The BEEP command produces a simple beep sound. It's often used as an alert or notification.
   - Example:
   - BEEP

2. **SOUND Statement:**
   - The SOUND statement allows you to generate more complex sounds by specifying frequency, duration, and other parameters.
   - Example (plays a simple melody):
   - SOUND 440, 500 ' Play A4 (440 Hz) for 500 milliseconds
   - SOUND 494, 500 ' Play B4 (494 Hz) for 500 milliseconds
   - SOUND 523, 500 ' Play C5 (523 Hz) for 500 milliseconds

Let's analyze the provided code snippet:

The SOUND statement in QB64 is used to generate simple sounds with specific frequencies and durations.

Each line represents a separate sound:

The first line (SOUND 440, 500) plays a sound at a frequency of 440 Hz (A4) for 500 milliseconds.

The second line (SOUND 494, 500) plays a sound at a frequency of 494 Hz (B4) for 500 milliseconds.

The third line (SOUND 523, 500) plays a sound at a frequency of 523 Hz (C5) for 500 milliseconds.

The duration of 500 milliseconds means that each sound will play for half a second.

When you run this code, you'll hear three distinct tones corresponding to the specified frequencies.

3. **PLAY Statement:**
   ◦ The PLAY statement lets you play music using a string notation similar to sheet music.

   ◦ Example:

   ◦ PLAY "T120 O4 E F G F E D C O5 C D E D C B A O4 A B C B A G F C E G F A B C E"

Let's analyze the provided PLAY statement:

PLAY "T120 O4 E F G F E D C O5 C D E D C B A O4 A B C B A G F C E G F A B C E"

The PLAY statement in QB64 is used to play music using a string notation similar to sheet music.

The provided string "T120 O4 E F G F E D C O5 C D E D C B A O4 A B C B A G F C E G F A B C E" represents musical notes and their durations.

Let's break down the string:

T120: Sets the tempo to 120 beats per minute.

O4: Octave 4 (middle octave).

Notes:

E, F, G, D, C, B, and A represent specific musical notes.

The order of these notes indicates the melody.

Durations:

The absence of a duration value means a default duration (usually a quarter note).

E, F, G, D, C, B, and A are played with the default duration.

O5: Octave 5 (one octave higher).

C, D, E, D, C, B, and A are played with the default duration.

G, F, C, E, G, F, A, B, and C are played with the default duration.

The entire string represents a musical sequence, and when executed, it will play the corresponding melody.

4. **Audio Synthesizer:**

   - QB64 provides an audio synthesizer that you can experiment with.

   - You can find examples and details on the **QB64 Wiki SOUND page**.

CHAPTER 22 - SCREEN COORDINATES - QB64

Screen coordinates refer to the position of pixels or text characters on the screen. In QB64, you can work with different screen modes, each having its own resolution and coordinate system.

Here are some key points about screen coordinates in QB64:

1. **Screen Modes:**
    - QB64 supports various screen modes, each with different resolutions and color capabilities.
    - Common screen modes include:
        - **Screen 0:** Text mode (80 columns x 25 rows).
        - **Screen 13:** Graphics mode with a resolution of 320 x 200 pixels and 256 colors.
        - **Screen 12:** Graphics mode with a resolution of 640 x 480 pixels and 16 colors.
        - And more...

2. **Coordinate System:**
    - In graphics modes (like Screen 13), the coordinate system starts from the top-left corner.
    - The top-left pixel has coordinates (0, 0), where the first value represents the horizontal position (column) and the second value

represents the vertical position (row).

- The bottom-right pixel has coordinates (width - 1, height - 1), where width and height are the dimensions of the screen.

3. **Mathematical Adjustments:**
   - When calculating coordinates, remember that the last pixel's position is one less than the screen dimensions.
   - For example, in Screen 13 (320 x 200), the valid coordinates range from (0, 0) to (319, 199).

4. **Drawing and Interaction:**
   - You can use commands like PSET to place a pixel at a specific coordinate.
   - For lines, rectangles, circles, and other shapes, you'll need to specify starting and ending coordinates.
   - Interaction with the screen (e.g., mouse input) also relies on screen coordinates.

SCREEN 0: Text-Mode

SCREEN 1: 320 x 200 Resolution, 4 Colors

SCREEN 2: 640 x 200 Resolution, Black and White

SCREEN 7: 320 x 200 Resolution, 16 Colors

SCREEN 8: 640 x 200 Resolution, 16 Colors

SCREEN 9: 640 x 350 Resolution, 16 Colors

SCREEN 10: 640 x 350 Resolution, Black and White

SCREEN 11: 640 x 480 Resolution, Black and White

SCREEN 12: 640 x 480 Resolution, 16 Colors

SCREEN 13: 320 x 200 Resolution, 256 Colors

CHAPTER 23 - MAKING A FUNCTION - QB64

Functions allow you to encapsulate a specific piece of code that performs a particular task. By defining your own functions, you can make your programs more modular, organized, and reusable.

Here's how you can create a simple function in QB64:

1. **Function Definition:**
   - Start by defining your function using the FUNCTION keyword.
   - Specify the function name, any parameters it accepts, and its return type (if any).

2. **Function Body:**
   - Inside the function, write the code that performs the desired operation.
   - In the example above, the function Multiply takes two integer parameters (a and b) and returns their product.

3. **Calling the Function:**
   - To use your function, call it from another part of your program.

4. **Testing and Refining:**
   - Run your program and verify that the function works as expected.
   - You can create additional functions for

different tasks and organize your code effectively.

CHAPTER 24 - TYPE EXAMPLE - QB64

Let's explore how to define custom types (also known as user-defined types) in QB64. A type allows you to create a structure that can hold multiple elements. Think of it as defining your own data structure with specific fields.

Here's how you can create and use a custom type in QB64:

```
' Define a custom type called "Person"

TYPE Person

    FirstName AS STRING

    LastName AS STRING

    Age AS INTEGER

END TYPE


' Declare variables of the custom type

DIM p1 AS Person

DIM p2 AS Person


' Assign values to the fields

p1.FirstName = "John"

p1.LastName = "Doe"

p1.Age = 30
```

p2.FirstName = "Alice"

p2.LastName = "Smith"

p2.Age = 25

' Display information about the persons

PRINT "Person 1:"

PRINT "Name: "; p1.FirstName; " "; p1.LastName

PRINT "Age: "; p1.Age

PRINT

PRINT "Person 2:"

PRINT "Name: "; p2.FirstName; " "; p2.LastName

PRINT "Age: "; p2.Age

In this example:

- We define a custom type called Person with three fields: FirstName, LastName, and Age.
- We declare two variables (p1 and p2) of type Person.
- We assign values to the fields for each person.
- Finally, we display information about both persons.

CHAPTER 25 – KEYWORD INDEX - QB64

The Keywords below were extracted from the QB64 app Keyword Help Index.

"These QBasic keywords (with a few noted exceptions) will work in all versions of QB64.

A

- *ABS (function) converts any negative numerical value to a positive value.*

- *CALL ABSOLUTE (statement) is used to access computer interrupt registers.*

- *ACCESS (file statement) sets the read and write access of a file when opened.*

- *ALIAS (QB64 DECLARE LIBRARY statement) denotes the actual name of an imported FUNCTION or SUB procedure.*

- *AND (logical operator) is used to compare two numerical values bitwise.*

- *AND (boolean) conditonal operator is used to include another evaluation in an IF...THEN or Boolean statement.*

- *APPEND (file mode) creates a new file or allows an existing file to have data added using WRITE (file statement) or PRINT (file statement)*

- AS is used to denote a variable type or file number.

- ASC (function) returns the ASCII code number of a text STRING character.

- ASC (statement) (QB64 only) sets the code value of an ASCII text character at a designated STRING position.

- ATN (function) or arctangent returns the angle in radians of a numerical TAN value.

B

- BEEP (statement) creates an error sound of a fixed duration.

- BINARY (file mode) creates or opens an existing file for GET and PUT byte-wise access.

- BLOAD (statement) transfers the contents of a BINARY BSAVE file to a specific Arrays.

- BSAVE (statement) transfers the contents of an Arrays to a specified size BINARY file.

- BYVAL (statement) assigns a numerical variable value by its value, not the name.

C

- CALL (statement) optional statement that sends the program to a SUB procedure. Requires parameters be enclosed in brackets(parenthesis).

- CALL ABSOLUTE (statement) is used to access computer interrupt registers.

- CASE (SELECT CASE condition) designates specific conditions in a SELECT CASE statement block.

- *CASE ELSE (SELECT CASE condition) designates an alternative condition to be evaluated in a SELECT CASE statement block.*

- *CASE IS (SELECT CASE condition) designates specific conditions in a SELECT CASE statement block.*

- *CDBL (function) returns the closest DOUBLE value of a number.*

- *CHAIN (statement) sends a program to another specified program module or compiled program.*

- *CHDIR (statement) changes the current program path for file access.*

- *CHR$ (function) returns a text STRING character by the specified ASCII code number.*

- *CINT (function) returns the closest INTEGER value of a numerical value.*

- *CIRCLE (statement) creates a circle, ellipse or arc at a designated graphical coordinate position.*

- *CLEAR (statement) sets all variable and array values to zero number values or empty STRINGs.*

- *CLNG (function) returns the closest LONG value of a numerical value.*

- *CLOSE (statement) closes specific file number(s) or all files when a number is not specified.*

- *CLS (statement) clears a program SCREEN, VIEW port or WINDOW.*

- *COLOR (statement) sets the current text foreground and/or background color to be used.*

- *COMMAND$ (function) returns the command line arguments passed when a program is run.*

- *COMMON (statement) sets a variable name as shared by CHAINed program modules.*

- *CONST (statement) sets a variable name and its value as a constant value to be used by all procedures.*

- COS (function) returns the cosine of a radian angle value.

- CSNG (function) returns the closest SINGLE value of a numerical value.

- CSRLIN (function) returns the present PRINT cursor text row SCREEN coordinate position.

- CVD (function) returns the DOUBLE numerical value of an 8 byte MKD$ STRING.

- CVDMBF (function) returns the DOUBLE numerical value of a MKDMBF$ STRING.

- CVI (function) returns the INTEGER numerical value of a 2 byte MKI$ STRING.

- CVL (function) returns the LONG numerical value of a 4 byte MKL$ STRING.

- CVS (function) returns the SINGLE numerical value of a 4 byte MKS $ STRING.

- CVSMBF (function) returns the SINGLE numerical value of a MKSMBF$ STRING.

D

- DATA (statement) creates a line of fixed program information separated by commas.

- DATE$ (function) returns the present Operating System date STRING formatted as mm-dd-yyyy.

- DATE$ (statement) sets the date of the Operating System using a mm-dd-yyyy STRING format.

- DECLARE (BASIC statement) declares a SUB or FUNCTION procedure at the start of a program. Not required in QB64.

- DECLARE LIBRARY declares a C++, SDL or Operating System SUB or FUNCTION to be used.

- *DECLARE DYNAMIC LIBRARY declares DYNAMIC, CUSTOMTYPE or STATIC library(DLL) SUB or FUNCTION.*

- *DEF SEG (statement) defines a segment in memory to be accessed by a memory procedure.*

- *DEFDBL (statement) defines a set of undefined variable name starting letters as DOUBLE type numerical values.*

- *DEFINT (statement) defines a set of undefined variable name starting letters as INTEGER type numerical values.*

- *DEFLNG (statement) defines a set of undefined variable name starting letters as LONG type numerical values.*

- *DEFSNG (statement) defines a set of undefined variable name starting letters as SINGLE type numerical values.*

- *DEFSTR (statement) defines a set of undefined variable name starting letters as STRING type values.*

- *DIM (statement) defines a variable as a specified type and can size a STATIC array.*

- *DO...LOOP (statement) sets a recursive procedure loop that can be ignored or exited using conditional arguments.*

- *DOUBLE (numerical type #) 8 byte value limited to values up to 15 decimal places.*

- *DRAW (statement) uses a special STRING format that draws graphical lines in specific directions.*

- *$DYNAMIC (Metacommand) used at the start of a program to set all program arrays as changeable in size using REDIM.*

E

- *ELSE (IF...THEN statement) is used to direct program flow when no other condition is evaluated as true.*

- *ELSEIF (IF...THEN statement) is used with THEN to set alternate conditional evaluations.*

- END (statement) sets the end of a program, sub-procedure, statement block, DECLARE LIBRARY or TYPE definition.

- IF...THEN (statement) ENDs an IF...THEN conditional block statement using more than one line of code.

- ENVIRON (statement) temporarily sets an environmental key/pair value.

- ENVIRON$ (function) returns a specified string setting or numerical position as an environmental STRING value.

- EOF (file function) returns -1 when a file INPUT (file statement) or GET has reached the end of a file.

- EQV (logic operator) is used to compare two numerical values bitwise.

- ERASE (statement) clears the values from $STATIC arrays and completely removes $DYNAMIC arrays.

- ERDEV (function) returns an error code from the last device to create an error.

- ERDEV$ (function) returns the 8 character name of the last device to declare an error as a STRING.

- ERL (error function) returns the closest line number before an error occurred if line numbers are used.

- ERR (function) returns the ERROR Codes when a program error occurs.

- ERROR (statement) sets a specific ERROR Code to be simulated.

- EVERYCASE Used on SELECT CASE statement.

- EXIT (statement) immediately exits a program FOR...NEXT, DO...LOOP, SUB or FUNCTION procedure.

- EXP (function) returns the value of e to the exponential power specified.

F

- FIELD (statement) defines the variable sizes to be written or read from a file.

- FILEATTR (function) returns the current file access mode.

- FILES (statement) returns a list of files in the current directory path to the SCREEN.

- FIX (function) returns the rounded INTEGER value of a numerical value.

- FOR...NEXT (statement) creates a recursive loop procedure that loop a specified number of times.

- FOR (file statement) used in an OPEN file or device statement to indicate the access mode.

- FRE (function) returns the number of bytes of Memory available to running programs.

- FREE (QB64 TIMER statement) frees a numbered TIMER event in QB64.

- FREEFILE (file function) returns a file number that is currently not in use by the Operating System.

- FUNCTION (procedure block) sub-procedure that can calculate and return one value to a program in its name.

G

- GET (file statement) reads a file sequencially or at a specific position and returns the value as the variable type used.

- GET (TCP/IP statement) reads a connection port to return a value.

- GET (graphics statement) maps an area the current SCREEN video information and places it in an INTEGER arrays.

- GOSUB (statement) sends the program to a designated line label *procedure in the main program.*

- GOTO (statement) sends the program to a designated line number or line label in a procedure.

H

- HEX$ (function) returns the hexadecimal (base 16) STRING representation of the INTEGER part of any value.

I

- IF...THEN (statement) a conditional block statement used control program flow.

- IMP (logic operator) is used to compare two numerical values bitwise.

- $INCLUDE (Metacommand) designates a text code library file to include with the program.

- INKEY$ (function) ASCII returns a STRING value entry from the keyboard.

- INP (function) returns a numerical value from a specified port register address. See Keyboard scancodes

- INPUT (statement) a user input that returns a value to one or more specified variable(s).

- INPUT (file mode) OPEN statement that only allows an existing file to be read using INPUT (file statement) or INPUT$.

- INPUT (file statement) reads a file sequentially using the variable types designated.

- INPUT$ (function) returns a designated number of STRING bytes from the keyboard entry or a file number.

- INSTR (function) returns the position in a text STRING where a character sequence match starts.

- *INT (function) rounds a numerical value to an INTEGER value by removing the decimal point fraction.*

- *INTEGER (% numerical type) 2 byte whole values from -32768 to 32767.*

- *INTERRUPT (statement) is used to access computer interrupt registers.*

- *INTERRUPTX (statement) is used to access computer interrupt registers.*

- *IOCTL (statement)*

- *IOCTL$ (function)*

K

- *KEY n (statement) used with ON KEY(n) events to assign a "softkey" string to a key or create a user defined key.*

- *KEY(n) (statement) used with ON KEY(n) events to assign, enable, disable or suspend event trapping.*

- *KEY LIST (statement) lists the 12 Function key soft key string assignments going down left side of screen.*

- *KILL (statement) deletes the specified file without a warning. Remove empty folders with RMDIR.*

L

- *LBOUND (function) returns the lower boundary of the specified array.*

- *LCASE$ (function) returns the lower case value of a STRING.*

- *LEFT$ (function) returns the specified number of text characters from the left end of a STRING.*

- *LEN (function) returns the length or number of characters in a STRING value in bytes.*

- LET (statement) assigns a variable a literal value. Not required.

- LINE (statement) creates a graphic line or box on the SCREEN.

- LINE INPUT (statement) user input can be any text character including commas and quotes as a STRING value only.

- LINE INPUT (file statement) returns an entire text file line and returns it as a STRING value.

- KEY LIST displays the current ON KEY(n) function key (F1 to F10) "soft key" settings.

- LOC (function) returns the present file byte position or number of bytes in the OPEN COM buffer.

- LOCATE (statement) sets the text cursor's row and column position for a PRINT or INPUT statement.

- LOCK (statement) restricts access to portions or all of a file by other programs or processes.

- LOF (function) returns the size of an OPEN file in bytes.

- LOG (function) returns the natural logarithm of a specified numerical value

- LONG (& numerical type) 4 byte whole values from -2147483648 to 2147483647.

- DO...LOOP (block statement) bottom end of a recursive DO loop.

- LPOS (function) returns the printer head position.

- LPRINT (statement) sends STRING data to the default LPT or USB printer.

- LPRINT USING (statement) sends template formatted text to the default LPT or USB printer.

- LSET (statement) left justifies the text in a string so that there are no leading spaces.

- LTRIM$ (function) returns a STRING value with no leading spaces.

M

- MID$ (function) returns a designated portion of a STRING.

- MID$ (statement) redefines existing characters in a STRING.

- MKD$ (function) returns an 8 byte ASCII STRING representation of a DOUBLE numerical value.

- MKDIR (statement) creates a new folder in the current or designated program path.

- MKDMBF$ (function) returns an 8 byte Microsoft Binary Format STRING representation of a DOUBLE numerical value.

- MKI$ (function) returns a 2 byte ASCII STRING representation of an INTEGER.

- MKL$ (function) returns a 4 byte ASCII STRING representation of a LONG numerical value.

- MKS$ (function) returns a 4 byte ASCII STRING representation of a SINGLE numerical value.

- MKSMBF$ (function) returns an 8 byte Microsoft Binary Format STRING representation of a DOUBLE numerical value.

- MOD (math operator) performs integer remainder division on a numerical value.

N

- NAME (statement) names an existing file name AS a new file name.

- NEXT (statement) bottom end of a FOR...NEXT counter loop to returns to the start or a RESUME error.

- NOT (logical operator) inverts the value of a logic operation or returns True when a boolean evaluation is False.

O

- *OCT$ (function) returns the octal (base 8) STRING representation of the INTEGER part of any value.*

- *OFF (event statement) turns off all ON event checking.*

- *ON COM(n) (statement) sets up a COM port event procedure call.*

- *ON ERROR (statement) sets up and activates an error event checking procedure call. Use to avoid program errors.*

- *ON KEY(n) (statement) sets up a keyboard key entry event procedure.*

- *ON PEN (statement) sets up a pen event procedure call.*

- *ON PLAY(n) (statement) sets up a PLAY event procedure call.*

- *ON STRIG(n) (statement) sets up a joystick button event procedure call.*

- *ON TIMER(n) (statement) sets up a timed event procedure call.*

- *ON UEVENT (statement) Not implemented in QB64.*

- *ON...GOSUB (statement) sets up a numerical event procedure call.*

- *ON...GOTO (statement) sets up a numerical event procedure call.*

- *OPEN (file statement) opens a file name for an access mode with a specific file number.*

- *OPEN COM (statement) opens a serial communication port for access at a certain speed and mode.*

- *OPTION BASE (statement) can set the lower boundary of all arrays to 1.*

- *OR (logic operator) is used to compare two numerical values bitwise.*

- *OR (boolean) conditonal operator is used to include an alternative evaluation in an IF...THEN or Boolean statement.*

- *OUT (statement) writes numerical data to a specified register port.*

- *OUTPUT (file mode) creates a new file or clears all data from an existing file to acess the file sequencially.*

P

- PAINT (statement) fills an enclosed area of a graphics SCREEN with a color until it encounters a specific colored border.

- PALETTE (statement) sets the Red, Green and Blue color attribute intensities using a RGB multiplier calculation.

- PALETTE USING (statement) sets the color intensity settings using a designated arrays.

- PCOPY (statement) swaps two designated memory page images when page swapping is enabled in the SCREEN statement.

- PEEK (function) returns a numerical value from a specified segment address in memory.

- PEN (function) returns requested information about the lightpen device used.

- PEN (statement) enables/disables or suspends event trapping of a lightpen device.

- PLAY(n) (function) returns the number of notes currently in the background music queue.

- PLAY (statement) uses a special STRING format that can produce musical tones and effects.

- PMAP (function) returns the physical or WINDOW view graphic coordinates.

- POINT (function) returns the color attribute number or 32 bit _RGB32 value.

- POKE (statement) writes a numerical value to a specified segment address in memory.

- POS (function) returns the current text column position of the text cursor.

- PRESET (statement) sets a pixel coordinate to the background color unless one is specified.

- *PRINT (statement) prints text STRING or numerical values to the SCREEN.*

- *PRINT (file statement) prints text STRING or numerical values to a file.*

- *PRINT USING (statement) prints a template formatted STRING to the SCREEN.*

- *PRINT USING (file statement) prints a template formatted STRING to a file.*

- *PSET (statement) sets a pixel coordinate to the current color unless a color is designated.*

- *PUT (file I/O statement) writes data sequencially or to a designated position using a variable value.*

- *PUT (TCP/IP statement) sends raw data to a user's connection handle.*

- *PUT (graphics statement) places pixel data stored in an INTEGER array to a specified area of the SCREEN.*

R
- *RANDOM (file mode) creates a file or opens an existing file to GET and PUT records of a set byte size.*

- *RANDOMIZE (statement) sets the random seed value for a specific sequence of random RND values.*

- *RANDOMIZE restarts the designated seed value's random sequence of values from the beginning.*

- *READ (statement) reads values from a DATA field. ACCESS READ is used with the OPEN statement.*

- *REDIM (statement) creates a new $DYNAMIC array or resizes one without losing data when _PRESERVE is used.*

- *REM (statement) or an apostrophe tells the program to ignore statements following it on the same line.*

- RESET (statement) closes all files and writes the directory information to a diskette before it is removed from a disk drive.

- RESTORE (statement) resets the DATA pointer to the start of a designated field of data.

- RESUME (statement) an ERROR Codes handling procedure exit that can send the program to a line number or the NEXT code line.

- RETURN (statement) returns the program to the code immediately following a GOSUB call.

- RIGHT$ (function) returns a specific number of text characters from the right end of a STRING.

- RMDIR (statement) removes an empty folder from the current path or the one designated.

- RND (function) returns a random number value from 0 to .9999999.

- RSET (statement) right justifies a string value so that any end spaces are moved to the beginning.

- RTRIM$ (function) returns a STRING with all spaces removed from the right end.

- RUN (statement) clears and restarts the program currently in memory or executes another specified program.

S

- SADD (function) returns the address of a STRING variable as an offset from the current data segment.

- SCREEN (function) can return the ASCII character code or color of the text at a text designated coordinate.

- SCREEN (statement) sets the display mode and size of the program window.

- SEEK (function) returns the present byte position in an OPEN file.

- SEEK (statement) moves to a specified position in an OPEN file.

- SELECT CASE (statement) a program flow block that can handle numerous conditional evaluations.

- SETMEM (function) sets the memory to use.

- SGN (function) returns -1 for negative, 0 for zero, and 1 for positive numerical values.

- SHARED (statement) designates that a variable can be used by other procedures or the main procedure when in a sub-procedure.

- SHELL (statement) sends STRING commands to the command line. SHELL calls will not affect the current path.

- SHELL (function) executes an external command or calls another program. Returns codes sent by END or SYSTEM.

- SIGNAL (OS 2 event)

- SIN (function) returns the sine of a radian angle.

- SINGLE (! numerical type) 4 byte floating decimal point values up to 7 decimal places.

- SLEEP (statement) pauses the program for a designated number of seconds or until a key is pressed.

- SOUND (statement) creates a sound of a specified frequency and duration.

- SPACE$ (function) returns a designated number of spaces to a STRING.

- SPC (function) moves the text cursor a number of spaces on the SCREEN.

- SQR (function) returns the square root of a non-negative number.

- STATIC (statement) creates a SUB or FUNCTION variable that retains its value.

- $STATIC (Metacommand) used at the start of a program to set all program arrays as unchangeable in size using DIM.

- *STEP (keyword) move relatively from one graphic position or change the counting increment in a FOR...NEXT loop.*

- *STICK (function) returns the present joystick position.*

- *STOP (statement) stops a program when troubleshooting or stops an ON event.*

- *STR$ (function) returns a STRING value of a number with a leading space when it is positive.*

- *STRIG (function) returns the joystick button press values when read.*

- *STRIG(n) (statement)*

- *STRING ($ variable type) one byte text variable with ASCII code values from 0 to 255.*

- *STRING$ (function) returns a designated number of string characters.*

- *SUB (procedure block) sub-procedure that can calculate and return multiple parameter values.*

- *SWAP (statement) swaps two STRING or numerical values.*

- *SYSTEM (statement) ends a program immediately.*

T

- *TAB (function) moves a designated number of columns on the SCREEN.*

- *TAN (function) returns the ratio of SINe to COSine or tangent value of an angle measured in radians.*

- *THEN (IF...THEN keyword) must be used in a one line IF...THEN program flow statement.*

- *TIME$ (function) returns the present time setting of the Operating System as a format hh:mm:ss STRING.*

- *TIMER (function) returns the number of seconds since midnight as a SINGLE value.*

- *TIMER (statement) events based on the designated time interval and timer number.*

- *TO indicates a range of numerical values or an assignment of one value to another.*

- *TYPE (definition) defines a variable type or file record that can include any STRING or numerical types.*

U

- *UBOUND (function) returns the upper-most index number of a designated arrays.*

- *UCASE$ (function) returns an uppercase representation of a specified STRING.*

- *UEVENT (statement) Not implemented in QB64.*

- *UNLOCK (statement) unlocks a designated file or portions of it.*

- *UNTIL (condition) evaluates a DO...LOOP condition until it is True.*

V

- *VAL (function) returns the numerical value of a STRING number.*

- *VARPTR (function) returns the segment pointer address in memory.*

- *VARPTR$ (function) returns the string value of a numerical value in memory.*

- *VARSEG (function) returns the segment address of a value in memory.*

- *VIEW (graphics statement) sets up a graphic view port area of the SCREEN.*

- *VIEW PRINT (statement) sets up a text viewport area of the SCREEN.*

W

- *WAIT (statement) waits until a vertical retrace is started or a*

SCREEN draw ends.

- WEND (statement) the bottom end of a WHILE...WEND loop.

- WHILE (condition) evaluates a DO...LOOP or WHILE...WEND condition until it is False.

- WHILE...WEND (statement) sets a recursive procedure loop that can only be exited using the WHILE conditional argument.

- WIDTH (statement) sets the text column and row sizes in several SCREEN modes.

- WINDOW (statement) maps a window size different from the program's window size.

- WRITE (screen I/O statement) prints variable values to the screen with commas separating each value.

- WRITE (file statement) writes data to a file with each variable value separated by commas.

X

- XOR (logic operator) is used to compare two numerical values bitwise.

QB64 specific keywords::

Keywords beginning with underscores are QB64 specific. To use them without the prefix, use $NOPREFIX. Also note that the underscore prefix is reserved for QB64 KEYWORDS only.

_A

- _ACCEPTFILEDROP (statement) turns a program window into a valid drop destination for dragging files from Windows Explorer.

- _ACOS (function) arccosine function returns the angle in radians based on an input COSine value range from -1 to 1.

- _ACOSH (function) Returns the nonnegative arc hyperbolic cosine of x, expressed in radians.

- _ALLOWFULLSCREEN (statement) allows setting the behavior of the ALT+ENTER combo.

- _ALPHA (function) returns the alpha channel transparency level of a color value used on a screen page or image.

- _ALPHA32 (function) returns the alpha channel transparency level of a color value used on a 32 bit screen page or image.

- _ASIN (function) Returns the principal value of the arc sine of x, expressed in radians.

- _ASINH (function) Returns the arc hyperbolic sine of x, expressed in radians.

- _ASSERT (statement) Performs debug tests.

- $ASSERTS (metacommand) Enables the _ASSERT macro

- _ATAN2 (function) Returns the principal value of the ATN of y/x, expressed in radians.

- _ATANH (function) Returns the arc hyperbolic tangent of x, expressed in radians.

- _AUTODISPLAY (statement) enables the automatic display of the screen image changes previously disabled by _DISPLAY.

- _AUTODISPLAY (function) returns the current display mode as true (-1) if automatic or false (0) if per request using _DISPLAY.

- _AXIS (function) returns a SINGLE value between -1 and 1 indicating the maximum distance from the device axis center, 0.

_B

- _BACKGROUNDCOLOR (function) returns the current SCREEN background color.

- _BIT (` numerical type) can return only signed values of 0 (bit off) *and -1 (bit on). Unsigned 0 or 1.*

- *_BLEND (statement) statement turns on 32 bit alpha blending for the current image or screen mode and is default.*

- *_BLEND (function) returns -1 if enabled or 0 if disabled by _DONTBLEND statement.*

- *_BLINK (statement) statement turns blinking colors on/off in SCREEN 0*

- *_BLINK (function) returns -1 if enabled or 0 if disabled by _BLINK statement.*

- *_BLUE (function) function returns the palette or the blue component intensity of a 32-bit image color.*

- *_BLUE32 (function) returns the blue component intensity of a 32-bit color value.*

- *_BUTTON (function) returns -1 when a controller device button is pressed and 0 when button is released.*

- *_BUTTONCHANGE (function) returns -1 when a device button has been pressed and 1 when released. Zero indicates no change.*

- *_BYTE (%% numerical type) can hold signed values from -128 to 127 (one byte or _BIT 8). Unsigned from 0 to 255.*

_C

- *_CAPSLOCK (function) returns -1 when Caps Lock is on*

- *_CAPSLOCK (statement) sets Caps Lock key state*

- *$CHECKING (QB64 C++ Metacommand) turns event error checking OFF or ON.*

- *_CEIL (function) Rounds x upward, returning the smallest integral value that is not less than x.*

- *_CINP (function) Returns a key code from $CONSOLE input*

- *_CLEARCOLOR (function) returns the current transparent color of* *an image.*

- _CLEARCOLOR (statement) sets a specific color index of an image to be transparent

- _CLIP (PUT (graphics statement) graphics option) allows placement of an image partially off of the screen.

- _CLIPBOARD$ (function) returns the operating system's clipboard contents as a STRING.

- _CLIPBOARD$ (statement) sets and overwrites the STRING value in the operating system's clipboard.

- _CLIPBOARDIMAGE (function) pastes an image from the clipboard into a new QB64 image in memory.

- _CLIPBOARDIMAGE (statement) copies a valid QB64 image to the clipboard.

- $COLOR (metacommand) includes named color constants in a program

- _COMMANDCOUNT (function) returns the number of arguments passed to the compiled program from the command line.

- _CONNECTED (function) returns the status of a TCP/IP connection handle.

- _CONNECTIONADDRESS$ (TCP/IP function) returns a connected user's STRING IP address value using the handle.

- $CONSOLE (QB64 Metacommand) creates a console window that can be used throughout a program.

- _CONSOLE (statement) used to turn a console window OFF or ON or to designate _DEST _CONSOLE for output.

- _CONSOLEINPUT (function) fetches input data from a $CONSOLE window to be read later (both mouse and keyboard)

- _CONSOLETITLE (statement) creates the title of the console window using a literal or variable STRING.

- _CONTINUE (statement) skips the remaining lines in a control block

(DO/LOOP, FOR/NEXT or WHILE/WEND)

- _CONTROLCHR (statement) OFF allows the control characters to be used as text characters. ON (default) can use them as commands.

- _CONTROLCHR (function) returns the current state of _CONTROLCHR as 1 when OFF and 0 when ON.

- _COPYIMAGE (function) copies an image handle value to a new designated handle.

- _COPYPALETTE (statement) copies the color palette intensities from one 4 or 8 BPP image to another image.

- _CV (function) converts any _MK$ STRING value to the designated numerical type value.

- _CWD$ (function) returns the current working directory as a STRING value.

_D

- _D2G (function) converts degrees to gradian angle values.

- _D2R (function) converts degrees to radian angle values.

- $DEBUG (metacommand) enables debugging features, allowing you to step through your code line by line

- DECLARE LIBRARY declares a C++, SDL or Operating System SUB or FUNCTION to be used.

- DECLARE DYNAMIC LIBRARY declares DYNAMIC, CUSTOMTYPE or STATIC library (DLL) SUB or FUNCTION.

- _DEFAULTCOLOR (function) returns the current default text color for an image handle or page.

- _DEFINE (statement) defines a range of variable names according to their first character as a data type.

- _DEFLATE$ (function) compresses a string

- _DELAY (statement) suspends program execution for a SINGLE

number of seconds.

- _DEPTHBUFFER (statement) enables, disables, locks or clears depth buffering.

- _DESKTOPHEIGHT (function) returns the height of the desktop (not program window).

- _DESKTOPWIDTH (function) returns the width of the desktop (not program window).

- _DEST (statement) sets the current write image or SCREEN page destination for prints or graphics.

- _DEST (function) returns the current destination screen page or image handle value.

- _DEVICE$ (function) returns a STRING expression listing a designated numbered input device name and types of input.

- _DEVICEINPUT (function) returns the _DEVICES number of an _AXIS, _BUTTON or _WHEEL event.

- _DEVICES (function) returns the number of input devices found on a computer system including the keyboard and mouse.

- _DIR$ (function) returns common paths in Windows only, like My Documents, My Pictures, My Music, Desktop.

- _DIREXISTS (function) returns -1 if the Directory folder name STRING parameter exists. Zero if it does not.

- _DISPLAY (statement) turns off the _AUTODISPLAY while only displaying the screen changes when called.

- _DISPLAY (function) returns the handle of the current image that is displayed on the screen.

- _DISPLAYORDER (statement) designates the order to render software, hardware and custom-opengl-code.

- _DONTBLEND (statement) statement turns off default _BLEND 32 bit _ALPHA blending for the current image or screen.

- _DONTWAIT (SHELL action) specifies that the program should not

wait until the shelled command/program is finished.

- _DROPPEDFILE (function) returns the list of items (files or folders) dropped in a program's window after _ACCEPTFILEDROP is enabled.

_E

- _ECHO (statement) used in conjunction with $IF for the precompiler.

- $ELSE (Pre-Compiler Metacommand) used in conjunction with $IF for the precompiler.

- $ELSEIF (Pre-Compiler Metacommand) used in conjunction with $IF for the precompiler.

- $END IF (Pre-Compiler Metacommand) used in conjunction with $IF for the precompiler.

- $ERROR (precompiler metacommand) used to trigger compiler errors.

- _ERRORLINE (function) returns the source code line number that caused the most recent runtime error.

- _ERRORMESSAGE$ (function) returns a human-readable message describing the most recent runtime error.

- $EXEICON (Pre-Compiler Metacommand) used with a .ICO icon file name to embed the image into the QB64 executable.

- _EXIT (function) prevents a user exit and indicates if a user has clicked the close X window button or CTRL + BREAK.

_F

- _FILEEXISTS (function) returns -1 if the file name STRING parameter exists. Zero if it does not.

- _FINISHDROP (statement) resets _TOTALDROPPEDFILES and clears the _DROPPEDFILE list of items (files/folders).

- _FLOAT (numerical type ##) offers the maximum floating-point

decimal precision available using QB64.

- _FONT (statement) sets the current font handle to be used by PRINT or _PRINTSTRING.

- _FONT (function) creates a new font handle from a designated image handle.

- _FONTHEIGHT (function) returns the current text or font height.

- _FONTWIDTH (function) returns the current text or font width.

- _FREEFONT (statement) releases the current font handle from memory.

- _FREEIMAGE (statement) releases a designated image handle from memory.

- _FREETIMER (function) returns an unused timer number value to use with ON TIMER(n).

- _FULLSCREEN (statement) sets the program window to full screen or OFF. Alt + Enter does it manually.

- _FULLSCREEN (function) returns the fullscreen mode in use by the program.

_G

- _G2D (function) converts gradian to degree angle values.

- _G2R (function) converts gradian to radian angle values.

- _GLRENDER (statement) sets whether context is displayed, on top of or behind the software rendering.

- _GREEN (function) function returns the palette or the green component intensity of a 32-bit image color.

- _GREEN32 (function) returns the green component intensity of a 32-bit color value.

_H

- _HEIGHT (function) returns the height of a designated image handle.

- _HIDE (SHELL action) hides the command line display during a shell.

- _HYPOT (function) Returns the hypotenuse of a right-angled triangle whose legs are x and y.

_I

- $IF (Pre-Compiler Metacommand) used to set an IF condition for the precompiler.

- _ICON (statement) designates a _LOADIMAGE image file handle to be used as the program's icon or loads the embedded icon (see $EXEICON).

- _INCLERRORFILE$ {function) returns the name of the original source code $INCLUDE module that caused the most recent error.

- _INCLERRORLINE (function) returns the line number in an included file that caused the most recent error.

- _INFLATE$ (function) decompresses a string

- _INSTRREV (function) allows searching for a substring inside another string, but unlike INSTR it returns the last occurrence instead of the first one.

- _INTEGER64 (&& numerical type) can hold whole numerical values from -9223372036854775808 to 9223372036854775807.

_K

- _KEYCLEAR (statement) clears the keyboard buffers for INKEY$, _KEYHIT, and INP.

- _KEYHIT (function) returns ASCII one and two byte, SDL Virtual Key and Unicode keyboard key press codes.

- _KEYDOWN (function) returns whether CTRL, ALT, SHIFT,

combinations and other keys are pressed.

_L

- *$LET (Pre-Compiler Metacommand) used to set a flag variable for the precompiler.*

- *_LASTAXIS (function) returns the number of axis available on a specified number device listed by _DEVICE$.*

- *_LASTBUTTON (function) returns the number of buttons available on a specified number device listed by _DEVICE$.*

- *_LASTWHEEL (function) returns the number of scroll wheels available on a specified number device listed by _DEVICE$.*

- *_LIMIT (statement) sets the loops per second rate to slow down loops and limit CPU usage.*

- *_LOADFONT (function) designates a _FONT TTF file to load and returns a handle value.*

- *_LOADIMAGE (function) designates an image file to load and returns a handle value.*

_M

- *_MAPTRIANGLE (statement) maps a triangular image source area to put on a destination area.*

- *_MAPUNICODE (statement) maps a Unicode value to an ASCII code number.*

- *_MAPUNICODE (function) returns the Unicode (UTF32) code point value of a mapped ASCII character code.*

- *_MEM (function) returns _MEM block referring to the largest continuous memory region beginning at a designated variable's offset.*

- *_MEM (variable type) contains read only dot elements for the OFFSET, SIZE, TYPE and ELEMENTSIZE of a block of memory.*

- _MEMCOPY (statement) copies a value from a designated OFFSET and SIZE TO a block of memory at a designated OFFSET.

- _MEMELEMENT (function) returns a _MEM block referring to a variable's memory (but not past it).

- _MEMEXISTS (function) verifies that a memory block exists for a memory variable name or returns zero.

- _MEMFILL (statement) fills a designated memory block OFFSET with a certain SIZE and TYPE of value.

- _MEMFREE (statement) frees a designated memory block in a program. Only free memory blocks once.

- _MEMGET (statement) reads a value from a designated memory block at a designated OFFSET

- _MEMGET (function) returns a value from a designated memory block and OFFSET using a designated variable TYPE.

- _MEMIMAGE (function) returns a _MEM block referring to a designated image handle's memory

- _MEMNEW (function) allocates new memory with a designated SIZE and returns a _MEM block referring to it.

- _MEMPUT (statement) places a designated value into a designated memory block OFFSET

- _SCREENMOVE (_SCREENMOVE parameter) centers the program window on the desktop in any screen resolution.

- _MK$ (function) converts a numerical value to a designated ASCII STRING value.

- _MOUSEBUTTON (function) returns the status of a designated mouse button.

- _MOUSEHIDE (statement) hides the mouse pointer from view

- _MOUSEINPUT (function) returns a value if the mouse status has changed since the last read.

- _MOUSEMOVE (statement) moves the mouse pointer to a designated position on the program SCREEN.

- _MOUSEMOVEMENTX (function) returns the relative horizontal position of the mouse cursor compared to the previous position.

- _MOUSEMOVEMENTY (function) returns the relative vertical position of the mouse cursor compared to the previous position.

- _MOUSEPIPEOPEN (function) creates a pipe handle value for a mouse when using a virtual keyboard.

- _MOUSESHOW (statement) displays the mouse cursor after it has been hidden or can change the cursor shape.

- _MOUSEWHEEL (function) returns the number of mouse scroll wheel "clicks" since last read.

- _MOUSEX (function) returns the current horizontal position of the mouse cursor.

- _MOUSEY (function) returns the current vertical position of the mouse cursor.

_N

- _NEWIMAGE (function) creates a designated size program SCREEN or page image and returns a handle value.

- $NOPREFIX (metacommand) allows QB64-specific keywords to be used without the underscore prefix.

- _NUMLOCK (function) returns -1 when Num Lock is on

- _NUMLOCK (statement) sets Num Lock key state

_O

- _OFFSET (function) returns the memory offset of a variable when used with DECLARE LIBRARY or _MEM only.

- _OFFSET (%& numerical type) can be used store the value of an offset in memory when using DECLARE LIBRARY or MEM only.

- _OPENCLIENT (TCP/IP function) connects to a Host on the Internet as a Client and returns the Client status handle.

- _OPENCONNECTION (TCP/IP function) open's a connection from a client that the host has detected and returns a status handle.

- _OPENHOST (TCP/IP function) opens a Host and returns a Host status handle.

- OPTION _EXPLICIT (Pre-compiler directive) instructs the compiler to require variable declaration with DIM or an equivalent statement.

- OPTION _EXPLICITARRAY (Pre-compiler directive) instructs the compiler to require array declaration with DIM or an equivalent statement.

- _OS$ (function) returns the QB64 compiler version in which the program was compiled as [WINDOWS], [LINUX] or [MACOSX] and [32BIT] or [64BIT].

_P

- _PALETTECOLOR (statement) sets the color value of a palette entry of an image using 256 colors or less palette modes.

- _PALETTECOLOR (function) return the 32 bit attribute color setting of an image or screen page handle's palette.

- _PI (function) returns the value of Ï€ or parameter multiples for angle or CIRCLE calculations.

- _PIXELSIZE (function) returns the pixel palette mode of a designated image handle.

- _PRESERVE (REDIM action) preserves the data presently in an array when REDIM is used.

- _PRINTIMAGE (statement) sends an image to the printer that is stretched to the current printer paper size.

- _PRINTMODE (statement) sets the text or _FONT printing mode on a background when using PRINT or _PRINTSTRING.

- _PRINTMODE (function) returns the present _PRINTMODE value number.

- _PRINTSTRING (statement) locates and prints a text STRING using graphic coordinates.

- _PRINTWIDTH (function) returns the pixel width of a text string to be printed using _PRINTSTRING.

- _PUTIMAGE (statement) maps a rectangular image source area to an image destination area.

_R

- _R2D (function) converts radians to degree angle values.

- _R2G (function) converts radians to gradian angle values.

- _RED (function) function returns the palette or the red component intensity of a 32-bit image color.

- _RED32 (function) returns the red component intensity of a 32-bit color value.

- _READBIT (function) returns the state of the specified bit of an integer variable.

- _RESETBIT (function) is used to set the specified bit of an integer variable to 0.

- $RESIZE (Metacommand) used with ON allows a user to resize the program window where OFF does not.

- _RESIZE (statement) sets resizing of the window ON or OFF and sets the method as _STRETCH or _SMOOTH.

- _RESIZE (function) returns -1 when a program user wants to resize the program screen.

- _RESIZEHEIGHT (function) returns the requested new user screen height when $RESIZE:ON allows it.

- _RESIZEWIDTH (function) returns the requested new user screen *width when $RESIZE:ON allows it.*

- _RGB (function) returns the closest palette index OR the LONG 32 bit color value in 32 bit screens.

- _RGB32 (function) returns the LONG 32 bit color value in 32 bit screens only

- _RGBA (function) returns the closest palette index OR the LONG 32 bit color value in 32 bit screens with the ALPHA

- _RGBA32 (function) returns the LONG 32 bit color value in 32 bit screens only with the ALPHA

- _ROUND (function) rounds to the closest INTEGER, LONG or _INTEGER64 numerical value.

_S

- _SCREENCLICK (statement) simulates clicking on a point on the desktop screen with the left mouse button.

- _SCREENEXISTS (function) returns a -1 value once a screen has been created.

- $SCREENHIDE ([QB64 [Metacommand]]) hides the program window from view.

- _SCREENHIDE (statement) hides the program window from view.

- _SCREENICON (function) returns -1 or 0 to indicate if the window has been minimized to an icon on the taskbar.

- _SCREENICON (statement) minimizes the program window to an icon on the taskbar.

- _SCREENIMAGE (function) creates an image of the current desktop and returns an image handle.

- _SCREENMOVE (statement) positions program window on the desktop using designated coordinates or the _MIDDLE option.

- _SCREENPRINT (statement) simulates typing text into a Windows

program using the keyboard.

- *$SCREENSHOW (QB64 Metacommand) displays that program window after it was hidden by $SCREENHIDE.*

- *_SCREENSHOW (statement) displays the program window after it has been hidden by _SCREENHIDE.*

- *_SCREENX (function) returns the program window's upper left corner horizontal position on the desktop.*

- *_SCREENY (function) returns the program window's upper left corner vertical position on the desktop.*

- *_SCROLLLOCK (function) returns -1 when Scroll Lock is on*

- *_SCROLLLOCK (statement) sets Scroll Lock key state*

- *_SETALPHA (statement) sets the alpha channel transparency level of some or all of the pixels of an image.*

- *_SETBIT (function) is used to set the specified bit of an integer variable to 1.*

- *_SHELLHIDE (function) returns the code sent by a program exit using END or SYSTEM followed by an INTEGER value.*

- *_SHL (function) used to shift the bits of a numerical value to the left*

- *_SHR (function) used to shift the bits of a numerical value to the right.*

- *Mathematical Operations (function) Returns the hyperbolic sine of x radians.*

- *_SNDBAL (statement) attempts to set the balance or 3D position of a sound file.*

- *_SNDCLOSE (statement) frees and unloads an open sound using the sound handle created by _SNDOPEN.*

- *_SNDCOPY (function) copies a sound handle value to a new designated handle.*

- *_SNDGETPOS (function) returns the current playing position in* seconds from a sound file.

- _SNDLEN (function) returns the length of a sound in seconds from a sound file.

- _SNDLIMIT (statement) stops playing a sound after it has been playing for a set number of seconds.

- _SNDLOOP (statement) plays a sound repeatedly until _SNDSTOP is used.

- _SNDOPEN (function) loads a sound file and returns a sound handle.

- _SNDOPENRAW (function) opens a new channel to shove _SNDRAW content into without mixing.

- _SNDPAUSE (statement) stops playing a sound file until resumed.

- _SNDPAUSED (function) returns the current pause status of a sound file handle.

- _SNDPLAY (statement) plays a sound file handle that was created by _SNDOPEN or _SNDCOPY.

- _SNDPLAYCOPY (statement) copies a sound handle, plays it and automatically closes the copy when done.

- _SNDPLAYFILE (statement) directly plays a designated sound file.

- _SNDPLAYING (function) returns the current playing status of a sound handle.

- _SNDRATE (function) returns the sound card sample rate to set _SNDRAW durations.

- _SNDRAW (statement) creates mono or stereo sounds from calculated wave frequency values.

- _SNDRAWDONE (statement) pads a _SNDRAW stream so the final (partially filled) buffer section is played.

- _SNDRAWLEN (function) returns a value until the _SNDRAW buffer is empty.

- _SNDSETPOS (statement) sets the playing position of a sound handle.

- _SNDSTOP (statement) stops playing a sound handle.

- _SNDVOL (statement) sets the volume of a sound file handle.

- _SOURCE (statement) sets the source image handle.

- _SOURCE (function) returns the present source image handle value.

- _STARTDIR$ (function) returns the user's program calling path as a STRING.

- _STRCMP (function) compares the relationship between two strings.

- _STRICMP (function) compares the relationship between two strings, without regard for case-sensitivity.

_T

- Mathematical Operations (function) Returns the hyperbolic tangent of x radians.

- _TITLE (statement) sets the program title STRING value.

- _TITLE$ (function) gets the program title STRING value.

- _TOGGLEBIT (function) is used to toggle the specified bit of an integer variable from 1 to 0 or 0 to 1.

- _TOTALDROPPEDFILES (function) returns the number of items (files or folders) dropped in a program's window after _ACCEPTFILEDROP is enabled.

- _TRIM$ (function) shorthand to LTRIM$(RTRIM$("text"))

_U

- _UNSIGNED (numerical type) expands the positive range of numerical INTEGER, LONG or _INTEGER64 values returned.

_V

- *$VERSIONINFO (Metacommand) adds metadata to Windows only binaries for identification purposes across the OS.*

- *$VIRTUALKEYBOARD (Metacommand - Deprecated) turns the virtual keyboard ON or OFF for use in touch-enabled devices*

_W

- *_WHEEL (function) returns -1 when a control device wheel is scrolled up and 1 when scrolled down. Zero indicates no activity.*

- *_WIDTH (function) returns the width of a SCREEN or image handle.*

- *_WINDOWHANDLE (function) returns the window handle assigned to the current program by the OS. Windows-only.*

- *_WINDOWHASFOCUS (function) returns true (-1) if the current program's window has focus. Windows-only."*

REFERENCES

- Olatunde Akano et al (2015), WABP Information and Communication Technology for JSS2

- J.O Otuka et al (2010) New Computer Studies for JSS1, Wole Olatokun et al (2007) Computer Studies for JSS2

- Vincent Hope et al (2015), WABP Computer Studies for SSS1 West African Book Publishers Ltd.

- J.O Otuka et al (2010) New Computer Studies for SSS1, Learn Africa Plc.

- Vincent Hope et al (2015), WABP Computer Studies for SSS2 West African Book Publishers Ltd.

- J.O Otuka et al (2010) New Computer Studies for SSS2, Learn Africa Plc.

- Vincent Hope et al (2015), WABP Computer Studies for SSS3 West African Book Publishers Ltd.

- J.O Otuka et al (2010) New Computer Studies for SSS3, Learn Africa Plc.

- Cory Smith, QB64: QB64.com

- Schoolfreeware Tutorials, SchoolFreeWare: schoolfreeware.com

www.ingramcontent.com/pod-product-compliance
Lightning Source LLC
LaVergne TN
LVHW051343050326
832903LV00031B/3716